an illustrated introduction to
THE STUARTS

Pamela Womack

Thanks go to the team at Amberley, and especially to Nicola and Christian for their support. Thanks also go to all of my family and friends for their encouragement, and particularly my son Peter, for his endless patience and help. Many thanks go to my dear friend Carol Dougherty, for her support and invaluable assistance with many of the illustrations.

The Execution of King Charles I before the Banqueting House, Whitehall, by Sir G. Kneller, *c.* 1786. (Author's collection)

First published 2014

Amberley Publishing
The Hill, Stroud
Gloucestershire, GL5 4EP

www.amberley-books.com

British Library Cataloguing in Publication Data.
A catalogue record for this book is available from the British Library.

ISBN 978 1 4456 3788 4 (paperback)
ISBN 978 1 4456 3800 3 (ebook)

Typesetting and Origination by Amberley Publishing.
Printed in Great Britain.

CONTENTS

THE STUARTS
IN FIVE MINUTES

Late on the evening of Saturday 26 March 1603, Sir Robert Carey, later 1st Earl of Monmouth, staggered, dishevelled, exhausted and injured, into the courtyard of Holyroodhouse Palace in Edinburgh. He had galloped at break-neck speed, desperate to be the first to bring the news of the death of Queen Elizabeth I, which had occurred two days earlier, to the Scottish king, James VI, who had long coveted Gloriana's throne.

Hurriedly wiping the sweat and blood from his face, and clutching in his shaking hand a blue ring entrusted to him by his sister, Lady Scrope, Lady-in-Waiting to the queen, as proof of Elizabeth's death, Carey was admitted to the king's chamber. Kneeling, he addressed his new monarch by the title of Sovereign of England, Scotland, France and Ireland. Although the Stuarts had long reigned in Scotland, it was the beginning of a new English dynasty; the Age of the Stuarts had begun.

The Stuart Age, encompassing the whole of the seventeenth century, was characterised by unprecedented change and turmoil; it was a century in which ordinary people lived through the most extraordinary events, and in which the lives of rich and poor alike were irrevocably changed. It was marked by religious wars between Protestants and Catholics in Europe and by religious unrest and conflict at home. Desperation, fear and anger, engendered by James I's refusal to ease the persecution of Roman Catholics, gave birth to the Gunpowder Plot in 1605, and fear and hatred of Popery would later result in the deposition of a Catholic monarch in favour of a foreign Protestant one.

The century witnessed the flourishing of art, architecture and literature, and saw huge advances in the field of scientific investigation, ushering in the beginning of the Age of Reason. By the end of the reign of the last Stuart monarch, England had emerged as a major world and European power.

Opposite: Charles I by Anthony van Dyck, *c.* 1635–37. (Author's collection)

James VI of Scotland, also crowned King James I of England, was the first Stuart to rule over the kingdoms of England, Scotland and Ireland. Dubbed 'the Wisest Fool in Christendom', James pursued his obsession for hunting and enjoyed infatuations with a series of gorgeous young male favourites, culminating in George Villiers, who was created 1st Duke of Buckingham. Shakespeare wrote the greatest of his tragedies during James's reign, while John Donne and Ben Jonson were part of a flourishing literary culture, and the king sponsored the translation of the Bible that bears his name, the Authorised King James Version, published in 1611. Francis Bacon laid the foundations for scientific experimentation and rational scientific thought, while Inigo Jones was commissioned to create the queen's house at Greenwich and the Banqueting House at Whitehall Palace.

Uncouth and bawdy, yet scholarly and with a fine intellect, James would survive his fear of witches and assassination only to die, prematurely aged, in 1625; he was sick in body and sick at heart at the failure of his pacifist foreign policy, when his favourite, Buckingham, and his son, Prince Charles, pushed the realm into war with Spain. James's great desire for a unified kingdom of Great Britain did not become a political reality until the reign of the last Stuart monarch, Queen Anne.

The beginning of Charles I's reign was characterised by conflict with Parliament. His refusal to allow the prosecution of his favourite, the unpopular Duke of Buckingham, led to the duke's assassination. Charles ruled for eleven years without calling Parliament, presiding over a court admired for its elegance, culture and formalised etiquette, and amassed a collection of art and sculptures unsurpassed in Europe. But unresolved political and religious tensions plunged the country into the horrors of the Civil Wars, when family loyalties were ripped apart, and which culminated in the unthinkable event of an anointed king being tried and executed by his own people.

The monarchy, the House of Lords and Episcopal Church were abolished, and for eleven years England became a Republic; a government in the name of the people was established, governed by Oliver Cromwell as Lord Protector.

The Protectorate did not survive Cromwell's death in 1658, and Charles II, cynical, clever, sensual and a born survivor, reclaimed the throne of the Royal Stuarts. During Charles's eventful reign, death stalked the streets of London as bubonic plague ravaged the population, claiming the lives of over 100,000 of his subjects, and fire ravaged and destroyed eighty percent of the Old City. From the charred ruins and ashes a new London arose, masterminded by Sir Christopher Wren. Coffee houses were opened, women performed on the stage for the first time, Samuel Pepys and John Evelyn wrote their diaries and John Milton wrote *Paradise Lost*. The introduction of the penny postal system in London in 1680 transformed communication, and the opposing political parties became known as Whigs and Tories for the first time. Charles's fascination with science led to the establishment of both the Royal Observatory in Greenwich and the Royal Society, led by such luminaries as Isaac Newton, Robert Hooke and Robert Boyle.

Nicknamed 'Old Rowley', after his favourite stud horse, Charles fathered thirteen illegitimate offspring, but his wife's inability to produce an heir plunged the country into crisis when his successor, his brother James, converted to Catholicism. Charles died in 1685, thinking of Nell Gwynne and apologising for taking so long to depart this life.

The Merry Monarch was succeeded by Dismal Jimmy. Autocratic and inflexible, James II's determination to promote Catholicism by appointing Catholics to military, political and academic posts, alarmed and alienated Parliament, the Church, the army, and even his own Protestant daughters, Mary – the wife of William of Orange – and Anne. The birth of a male Catholic heir in 1688 led to an invitation from a group of leading peers asking William of Orange, who had a claim to the throne, to invade the country as a champion of Protestantism. James fled to France, and, after being defeated by William at the Battle of the Boyne two years later, he spent the rest of his life in exile.

The Glorious Revolution of 1688 culminated in the crown being offered to William of Orange and his wife, Mary, the eldest daughter of James II, but the Bill of Rights imposed strict limits on royal power. After the death of the popular Mary in 1694, William ruled alone. The Bank of England was founded in the same year, to control public expenditure and fund the costly war with Louis XIV. Substantial constitutional changes culminated in the Act of Settlement in 1701, ensuring a Protestant succession. The Peace of Rijswijk in 1697 marked the end of the war with France, but the country was once more moving towards war by the time of William's death in 1702.

The twelve-year reign of Queen Anne witnessed the military successes of the Duke of Marlborough and the literary and architectural geniuses of Locke, Pope, Swift, Defoe and Vanbrugh. In 1707, the Act of Union ended the constitutional separation of England and Scotland. Overweight, conscientious and plagued by ill-health, the queen's fondness for brandy earned her the nickname 'Brandy Nan', and her fondness for gambling led to the establishment of the Ascot races. In her personal life, Anne suffered the pain of the loss of all her children and the breakdown of her intense friendship with Sarah Churchill while enduring the constant power struggle between Whig and Tory factions. Her death in 1714 signalled the end of an era and the beginning of the House of Hanover.

TIMELINE & FAMILY TREE

- **1603**
  Death of Queen Elizabeth I and accession of James VI of Scotland as James I of England.
- **1604**
  The Hampton Court Conference. Treaty of London ends war with Spain.
- **1605**
  Gunpowder Plot discovered. Measures passed against recusants.
- **1606**
  Royal proclamation that all British ships carry a new Union Jack.
- **1607**
  Foundation of first permanent English colony at Jamestown, Virginia.
- **1611**
  Publication of the King James Bible.
- **1612**
  Death of Prince Henry.
- **1616**
  Death of William Shakespeare.
- **1618**
  Beginning of the Thirty Years' War. Execution of Sir Walter Raleigh.
- **1619**
  Death of Queen Anne.
- **1620**
  Pilgrim Fathers establish a colony at Plymouth, New England.
- **1623**
  Visit of Prince Charles and Buckingham to Madrid.
- **1625**
  Death of James I and accession of Charles I. Marriage by proxy of Charles I and Henrietta Maria.
- **1627**
  England declares war on France. Failure of Buckingham's expeditionary force to aid French Huguenots at La Rochelle.
- **1628**
  The Petition of Right. Assassination of the Duke of Buckingham.
- **1629**
  Beginning of Personal Rule.
- **1638**
  The National Covenant.
- **1641**
  The Grand Remonstrance.
- **1642–5**
  Civil War.
- **1648**
  Pride's Purge.
- **1649**
  Execution of Charles I on 30 January.
- **1650**
  Cromwell fights in Ireland.
- **1651**
  Navigation Act.
- **1652–4**
  War against the Dutch.
- **1656–9**
  War against Spain.

1658
Death of Oliver Cromwell, succeeded by Richard Cromwell as Lord Protector.

1660
Restoration of Charles II.

1660–65
The Clarendon Code.

1660–9
Samuel Pepys writes his diary.

1665–7
War against the Dutch.

1665
The Great Plague.

1666
The Great Fire of London.

1672–4
War against the Dutch.

1685
Death of Charles II and accession of James II.

1688
Birth of James Francis Edward to James II and Mary of Modena. The Glorious Revolution.

1689–97
William of Orange and Mary accept the offer of joint sovereignty and are crowned as William III and Mary II. War against France.

1690
Battle of the Boyne.

1694
Death of Mary II.

1702
Death of William III and accession of Queen Anne.

1702–13
War of the Spanish Succession.

1704
Battle of Blenheim.

1707
The Act of Union.

1714
Death of Queen Anne and accession of George I.

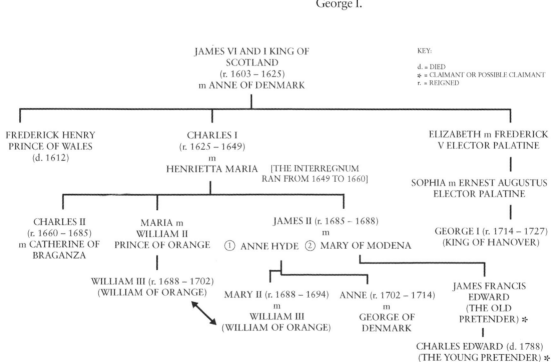

1
JAMES I
1603–1625

THE LAND OF PROMISE

On Sunday 3 April 1603, a jubilant King James VI of Scotland made his last public appearance in the country of his birth, attending divine service at St Giles's Church in Edinburgh. After the service, James bade an emotional and eloquent farewell and, despite assuring his sorrowing people that he would return every three years, it would be 1617 before their king would set foot again upon Scottish soil. Two days later, James departed for the new kingdom for which he had waited so long, leaving his wife and children to follow later. The king feasted and hunted all the way to London and his English subjects flocked to catch a glimpse of their new monarch.

They would have seen a man of middling height, with reddish-brown hair, a thin, straggly beard and a ruddy complexion. A life-long fear of assassination led to his wearing of thickly padded doublets, which made him appear more corpulent than he really was. Although the king's tongue was rather large for his mouth and his legs were weak, he was hardly the slobbering, uncouth caricature penned by the vengeful courtier, Sir Anthony Weldon, which has been generally accepted.

Queen Elizabeth I had slipped peacefully into death in the early hours of 24 March 1603 at her Palace of Richmond, and the people of London awoke to the news that, after forty-five years, there was again a king on the throne of England: James VI of Scotland, Elizabeth's first cousin, twice removed. James's accession was generally unquestioned and unresisted, and he was greeted with joy and relief by most of his new subjects, who regarded a male Protestant king with several children as offering security and a stable succession.

Opposite: James VI of Scotland as a child. Unknown artist. (Courtesy of Rijksmuseum, Amsterdam)

Far left: Sir Robert Carey's Ride by George Browne. Sir Robert Carey, later 1st Earl of Monmouth, galloped at break-neck speed to bring the news of the death of Queen Elizabeth I to James VI of Scotland at Holyroodhouse Palace in Edinburgh. (Author's collection)

Left: King James I. (Author's collection)

A CRADLE KING

James Stuart was born on 19 June 1566 at Edinburgh Castle, the son of the devoutly Catholic Mary, Queen of Scots, and her second husband, Henry Stuart, Lord Darnley. Darnley was murdered on 10 February 1567 in mysterious circumstances and his wife was suspected of being implicated in his death. Her marriage shortly afterwards to James Hepburn, 4th Earl of Bothwell, increased her unpopularity and in June 1567 Protestant rebels arrested Mary and imprisoned her in Loch Leven Castle.

The queen was forced to abdicate on 24 July 1567 in favour of her son, whom she never saw again, and her illegitimate half-brother, James Stewart, Earl of Moray, was appointed as regent. Scholarly and studious, James Stuart had an unstable and lonely childhood under a harsh regime of strict Protestant teachings. The survivor of kidnapping and assassination plots, James grew to manhood deeply mistrustful of others and determined to assert what he believed was his God-given authority.

On 25 July, the day of St James the Apostle, the new king, with his wife Anne of Denmark beside him, was crowned James I in Westminster Abbey. James had been King of Scotland for thirty-six years and had enjoyed a relatively successful reign, skilfully balancing the different factions of the Scottish nobility and leaders of the Kirk (Scottish Church). Canny and wily, and possessing an adaptable political mind, all his experience and considerable negotiating skills were required in order to govern his new realm, for Elizabeth had bequeathed him not only her crown but several serious challenges.

Above left: James I by Nicholas Hilliard, *c.* 1610. (Yale Center for British Art, Paul Mellon Fund)

Above right: Anne of Denmark by the studio of Nicholas Hilliard, after 1574. (Yale Center for British Art, Paul Mellon Fund)

THE BRITISH KINGDOMS

James's first problem was a new one: he was now not only ruler of the multiple kingdoms of England, Wales and Ireland, but of Scotland as well; each kingdom had its own distinctive culture, religious structure and government institutions. Wales had been conquered before 1500, and had been incorporated into the English kingdom by three Acts of Union passed in the reign of Henry VIII. England was governed by a monarch, assisted by a Privy Council, a system of law courts and the occasional meeting of Parliament. Scotland had its Parliament in Edinburgh, a Church Assembly and a Scottish Privy Council. Ireland was governed by a Lord Deputy and had its own Parliament which met in Dublin. In 1502, Henry VII had arranged a marriage between his daughter Margaret and James IV of Scotland, desiring to bring the two kingdoms together. However, the aggressive policies of his son, Henry VIII, had ensured that traditional hostilities continued, which encouraged the Scots to maintain an alliance with France.

James's accession as ruler of both kingdoms ended national hostilities, but there were deep-seated cultural differences, a bitter legacy of warfare and the

Leather and oak dice shaker and a bone dice with solid dots or 'pips' on a Long Lawrence, which was a form of long dice made from oak, described by Francis Willughby in his *Book of Games* in the mid-seventeenth century. It was used for playing the game of Put and Take, a well-known and ancient children's game. (Author's collection. Courtesy of Gothic Green Oak and The Historic Games Shop)

memories of English attempts to conquer Scotland in the thirteenth and fourteenth centuries. James wished to unite England and Scotland as the kingdom of Great Britain, with a common Parliament, government and laws, claiming that 'I am the Husband and all the whole Isle is my lawful wife'.

However, there were fears that the interests of one country would be subordinated to those of the others. The English Parliament did not share their new king's enthusiasm for *unus rex*, *unus grex*, *una lex* (one king, one people, one law); they feared that religious differences, traditions and national antagonisms might disrupt political stability. The addition of many Scotsmen to court was resented and increased dissatisfaction.

Similarly, the Scots wished to maintain their laws, and they were concerned that the purity of the reformed Kirk might be compromised by the Church in England. Although James grandly proclaimed himself 'King of Great Britain' in October 1604, the union did not become a political reality until 1707 during the reign of Queen Anne, the last of the Stuart monarchs.

RELIGIOUS TENSIONS

The problems of ruling different kingdoms were made more difficult and complex by religious divisions. The 'Elizabethan Settlement' of 1559 had established

England as a Protestant country with a national church, with the monarch, not the Pope, as its head. Services, which were held in every parish church, followed the Book of Common Prayer and were attended by everyone. Those who refused, known as recusants, were fined, imprisoned and occasionally even executed.

The settlement was intended as a compromise between Catholic and Protestant extremes and, although Protestant in doctrine, it retained many of the ceremonies inherited from the Catholic Church, as well as the role of bishops. By 1603 England was broadly a Protestant nation, united by a fear of Catholicism. Puritans were a minority within the church who desired that there should be further reform. The majority of Catholics were loyal to the Crown and posed little threat to the State by 1603.

In Scotland, the Presbyterian Church dominated the lowland areas. Presbyterianism was a form of Protestantism, established by the reformer John Knox and based on the teachings of John Calvin, who believed in the concept of pre-destination; this was the belief that God ordained salvation for some people and damnation for others, and it demanded that its followers adhered to a strict code of conduct. A notable minority of Catholics remained in the Gaelic highlands.

In Ireland, the majority of the population were Catholic, but English control had imposed the Anglican Church as the official Church of Ireland and Protestant settlers followed an extreme tradition of Presbyterianism.

Hopes that, as a devout Protestant with an upbringing in the strict Presbyterian Kirk of Scotland, James might favour further reform in the Church encouraged Puritans to present the king with the 'Millenary Petition'. This led to the Hampton Court Conference in 1604, but James rejected their ideas and warned them that if they did not conform to the rules and doctrines of the Prayer Book, he would 'harry them out of the kingdom'. An able theologian, James ordered a new translation of the Bible which became known as the Authorised King James's Version of the Bible, published in 1611.

Catholics had hoped that respect for his Catholic mother, Mary Queen of Scots, would encourage the new king to ease persecution. Fairly tolerant in religious matters, James suspended the collection of finances for recusancy, but, faced with complaints of leniency in Parliament and the loss of income, he imposed them once again. The ensuing Gunpowder Plot of 1605 resulted in strict penalties being imposed on Roman Catholics.

Guy Fawkes. (Courtesy of St Peter's School, York)

FINANCES

James inherited a debt of around £300,000, brought about by inflation and Elizabeth's sales of Crown land to finance the war with Spain. She had also failed to update tax assessments in line with inflation, so that the king received much less than was intended when Parliament granted extra taxes. Furthermore, as a married man with a family, with three households to maintain – his own, the queen's and that of the Prince of Wales – the king required around £80,000 more than his unmarried predecessor. The situation was greatly exacerbated by James's extravagance; he overestimated the wealth of his new kingdom and was over-generous to friends and favourites. Although Robert Cecil, Earl of Salisbury, oversaw a vigorous reform programme including the Great Contract of 1610, the king's debts continued to rise.

EARLY PARLIAMENTS

In *The True Law of Free Monarchies* in 1598, James had written that 'the King is above the law'. The claim that kings were appointed by God and ruled in his name was not new, but his claim that the monarch was above the law and that his subjects' liberties existed solely by his goodwill, not by right, caused some apprehension.

James did little to put this into effect except to dissolve Parliament if he felt it was encroaching on his royal prerogative, both in 1614 and later in 1621, but again, this was nothing new; Queen Elizabeth I had done the same. However, James's fondness for delivering long, rambling lectures to Parliament provoked indignation. Nor did he appreciate the need to manage and direct Parliament in the skilful way Elizabeth had; he merely expected it to respond to his will.

The king's failure to influence the choice of Speaker, and his failure to ensure that the Commons included a number of Privy Councillors capable of directing matters away from controversial subjects, meant that Parliamentary sessions were dominated by disputes over MPs' rights and privileges, finances and the royal prerogative.

POCAHONTAS (C. 1595–1617)

Pocahontas, born Matoaka and known as Amonute, was the daughter of Chief Powhatan, who lived in the Tidewater region of Virginia. A famous story tells that she saved the life of Englishman John Smith, who had been captured in 1607, by placing her head upon his own when her father raised his war club to execute him.

Pocahontas was captured by the English during Anglo-Indian hostilities in 1613 and held for ransom, during which time she converted to Christianity, taking the name Rebecca. Rather than return to her own people, she chose to remain, and married tobacco planter John Rolfe, bearing him a son, Thomas Rolfe.

On 22 June 1616, the courtier John Chamberlain wrote of the arrival of Pocahontas and her husband in London, along with Thomas Dale, governor of Jamestown and 'some ten or twelve old and young'. She was later presented to the king on Twelfth Night, 6 January 1617, during the masque *The Vision of Delight* at the Banqueting House and Chamberlain wrote that she was returning to Virginia, although 'sore against her will'.

Pocahontas never reached Virginia. She died at Gravesend in March 1617, where she was buried at St George's church.

A HUNTING KING AND A DANCING QUEEN

James I's court was viewed by some contemporaries, and by later historians, as decadent and corrupt. James's habit of peppering his speech with bawdy and coarse oaths met with the disapproval of many, including Prince Henry, the heir to the throne. Restless and easily bored, the king moved his court incessantly, indulging his passion for hunting to the full, while the queen, who lived apart from her husband, was thought to be frivolous and extravagant.

James's fondness for handsome, young, male favourites was another cause of dissension, as they were the source of favour and patronage and the object of political manoeuvring. The king bestowed wealth and titles upon his favourites and two were of particular significance; these were Robert Carr, 1st Earl of Somerset, and George Villiers, 1st Duke of Buckingham. The exact nature of James's intense relationships with his favourites, particularly with Villiers, caused concern and disapproval and fuelled gossip both at home and abroad.

GEORGE VILLIERS, FIRST DUKE OF BUCKINGHAM (1592–1628)

George Villiers was introduced to James I in 1614 as a means of toppling Robert Carr, Ist Earl of Somerset, with his Catholic and pro-Spanish connections. The son of a minor gentleman, Villiers swiftly rose from being a cup-bearer to the king to being created Duke of Buckingham in 1623. The last and greatest of the royal favourites, Buckingham's great wealth, power and stranglehold over the king's favour and patronage caused resentment, while his relationship with James was the subject of many libellous satires and songs, such as the one below:

> To Buckingham
> The King loves you, you him
> Both love the same
> You love the King, he you
> Both buck-in-game.
> In game the King loves sport
> Of sports the buck
> Of all men you; and you
> Solely for your look.

FOREIGN POLICY

James viewed himself as a *rex pacificus* (peacemaker king) and his motto, 'Blessed are the peacemakers', typified his approach to foreign policy; he preferred diplomacy to war. In 1604 he had ended the war with Spain under the terms of the Treaty of London. His intention was to balance the marriage of his daughter Elizabeth to the German Protestant prince, Frederick V, Elector Palatine, by securing a marriage of the heir to the throne, Prince Henry, to the Spanish Infanta, daughter of the Catholic king, Philip III. After the sudden death of Prince Henry in 1612, James intended that his second son, Charles, would marry the Infanta.

The outbreak of the Thirty Years War of 1618–1648 in Europe transformed the situation. James's son-in-law Frederick was defeated at the Battle of the White Mountain in 1620 and was expelled from the throne of Bohemia, to which he had been elected by Protestant rebels of the Emperor; he fled from his homeland in the Palatine, along with James's daughter Elizabeth and their young family.

Demands by many Members of Parliament for military intervention, as well as financial pressures, forced James to summon Parliament in 1621. However, when the House of Commons tried to debate wider aspects of foreign policy and asserted their right to discuss any subject, he dissolved it.

LATER YEARS

By 1623 James's health was declining. Plagued by gout and crippled by arthritis, he was more dependent on Buckingham than ever, and reluctantly agreed to a mad-cap scheme devised by the favourite and Prince Charles for the two to travel incognito to Spain in an attempt to hasten the marriage negotiations between the Prince and the Infanta Maria Anna, sister of Philip IV. The discovery of the departure of the heir to the throne was greeted with disbelief and horror by Parliament and the populace, amid fears that he would be held hostage.

Charles and Buckingham returned home several months later, frustrated and insulted by their lack of success and what they perceived as dishonest dealing on the part of the Spanish king and his ministers.

KING JAMES, STEENIE AND BABY CHARLES

After James's initial jubilation at having his son and favourite safely home again, the ageing and increasingly infirm king was dominated and bullied by Buckingham

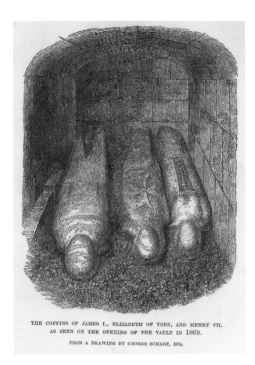

THE COFFINS OF JAMES I., ELIZABETH OF YORK, AND HENRY VII.
AS SEEN ON THE OPENING OF THE VAULT IN 1869.

FROM A DRAWING BY GEORGE SCHARF, ESQ.

The coffins of James I, Elizabeth of York and Henry VII as seen on the opening of the vault in 1869, from a drawing by George Scharf. Charles I's plans for a magnificent memorial to his father never materialised and for many years the whereabouts of the king's remains was unknown. In the nineteenth century, an extensive search revealed that James was laid in the vault beneath Henry VII's monument and lies next to Elizabeth of York and Henry VII. (Author's collection)

and Charles, who were now determined to break the hugely unpopular marriage treaty and were pushing for war with Spain, with Parliament's backing. Deeply unhappy, James finally capitulated with tears in his eyes, saying, 'Do you want me to go to war, in my twilight years, and force me to break with Spain?'

Believing that England needed an alliance with France, Buckingham negotiated a marriage for Charles with Henrietta Maria, the sister of the French Catholic king, Louis XIII. When the marriage treaty was ratified in December 1624, James's arthritis was so severe that he was unable to sign with his own hand and had to use a stamp.

DEATH OF SOLOMON

On 27 March 1625, James I died at his palace of Theobalds, aged fifty-eight, amid damaging but highly unlikely rumours of his being poisoned by Buckingham and his mother, in which Charles was implicated.

The label 'the wisest fool in Christendom', often attributed to Henry IV of France but written by Anthony Weldon, was never actually said, and scarcely does justice to the abilities and achievements of the first Stuart monarch.

2
CHARLES I
1625–1649

THE WHITE KING

On the afternoon of Friday 9 February 1649, a small, solemn funeral procession slowly approached St George's Chapel at Windsor. Holding the four corners of the pall were the Duke of Richmond, the Marquis of Hertford, the Earl of Lindsey and the Earl of Southampton, their faces as grey and sombre as the sky, from which fell heavy flakes of snow. The aged Bishop William Juxon walked behind the coffin of his dead master, Charles I, carrying a closed Book of Common Prayer; behind him followed the king's servants, including Sir Thomas Herbert and the Parliamentarian Colonel Whitchcott.

By the time the forlorn group had entered the west doors of the chapel, the black velvet pall was white with snow, a poignant reminder that, unusually, Charles had worn white, the colour of innocence, at his coronation rather than the usual purple. The text chosen for that sermon had been 'Be thou faithful unto death, and I will give thee a crown of life'.

Parliament had decreed that the slain king must not lie with his family in Henry VII's chapel at Westminster Abbey, fearing that his tomb might become a place of pilgrimage, and chose instead the less accessible St George's Chapel.

The cheap coffin, upon which Richmond had hastily scratched the king's name and the date, was lowered into a darkened vault containing the remains of Henry VIII and Jane Seymour and the velvet pall thrown down over it. Bishop Juxon, who had attended the king on the scaffold, had been refused permission to read the service for the dead, and so this most devout son of the Anglican Church was interred in silence, with no audible prayers for his eternal well-being and none of the ceremony which had played such a central role in his life.

As the grieving friends left their royal master, his meditations in captivity were published as *Eikon Basilike*, and so began the cult of the Martyr king.

Above: *The Funeral of King Charles I* by Allan Stewart. (Author's collection)

Left: The choir of St George's Chapel, Windsor, showing the memorial stone over the vault containing the body of Charles I. (Author's collection)

A SICKLY CHILD

Charles Stuart, Duke of Albany, was born at Dunfermline Palace, Fife, on 19 November 1600. The second son and fourth child born to James VI of Scotland and his wife Anne of Denmark was frail and unhealthy. It was not until his fourth year that he could walk unaided, and even in 1605 his legs were so weak that he had to be carried during the ceremony of his creation as Duke of York.

Through dogged perseverance, the young prince gradually overcame the weakness in his legs, becoming a fine, elegant rider. Charles displayed a similar determination to master a profound speech impediment which had greatly delayed his ability to talk, although he retained a life-long tendency to stammer when under stress.

Small and slight, with a pale, sensitive face, Charles compared unfavourably with his elder brother, the charismatic Henry Frederick, Prince of Wales. Six years older than Charles, Henry was handsome, muscular and athletic, the pride of his parents and the country. Charles idolised his brother, admiring his physical prowess, his devotion to the Protestant faith and his abstemious, serious demeanour; he regarded him as a role model, although he himself exceeded his brother in scholarly pursuits. Henry disapproved of swearing, drunkenness and his father's proclivity for handsome, perfumed young favourites, and a growing rivalry developed between the court of the popular, dashing prince and the decadent court of the king.

PRINCE OF WALES

Imbued from childhood with his father's belief in the Divine Right of kings, Charles never resented his elder brother's right to be the next king. However, in 1612 the glowingly vital Henry died, probably from typhoid, and the twelve year old Charles found himself the heir apparent and chief mourner at his adored brother's funeral. His sorrow and loneliness were compounded by the departure four months later of his beloved sister Elizabeth, after her marriage to Frederick V, Elector Palatine. Charles never saw her again.

Shy, serious and in awe of his father, Charles remained in the background at court, taking little part in political life. At first, he had detested the king's greatest favourite and probable lover, the impossibly handsome, flamboyant George Villiers, Earl of Buckingham, who had first place in his father's heart. However, he was won over by Buckingham's overwhelming charm and charisma, calling him by his father's pet name, 'Steenie', and the friendship became the most important of his life.

Charles I when Prince of Wales. Attributed to Peter Oliver, 1618–1621. (Courtesy of Yale Center for British Art, Paul Mellon Fund)

THE SPANISH MATCH

Charles was shocked and distressed when, in November 1620, the army of his brother-in-law Frederick was destroyed at the Battle of White Mountain, west of Prague, forcing Frederick, Elizabeth and their children into exile. The desire to enlist Spanish aid to help his sister and Frederick regain their home contributed to the hare-brained scheme devised by himself and Buckingham to travel incognito to Madrid, to personally supervise and hasten the arrangements for his marriage to the Infanta Maria Anna, the sister of Philip IV of Spain.

Initially horrified at the thought of his son, 'Baby Charles', and his favourite, 'Sweet Steenie', embarking upon such a risky venture, King James reluctantly agreed. Accordingly, in February 1623 the two young men, heavily disguised and using the names Tom and Jack Smith, set off on what must have seemed to them like a romantic adventure.

They returned in October in a very different humour, insulted and angry at what they regarded as the intransigence and dishonesty of the Spaniards, disgusted by the attempts to convert the prince to Catholicism and champing at the bit for war with Spain. The time abroad had deepened Charles's affection for and dependency on Buckingham, now a duke, and he was prepared to stand up to his father and refuse to marry the Infanta.

Prematurely aged and sick, James was unable to withstand the browbeating of his newly confident son and Buckingham, who had gained the support of Parliament. The last two years of his reign saw the country lurching towards a war he did not want, while the powerful Buckingham orchestrated another marriage alliance with Henrietta Maria, the sister of Louis XIII of France.

A KING AT WAR

Charles became king in March 1625. He and Buckingham expected Parliamentary support for the war with Spain, but to the king's surprise and chagrin, Parliament refused to vote the new monarch tonnage and poundage (customs duties) for life, as was usual, but merely for one year. Greatly insulted, Charles was also perplexed and angered at the hostility directed at his favourite, Buckingham, which he took personally. The duke was deeply unpopular and there was great concern that he appeared to have increased his power and influence over the young king.

Not only was Charles at loggerheads with Parliament, but his relationship with his queen, the devoutly Catholic Henrietta Maria, had deteriorated to the point where neither could bear the sight of the other. Tensions with Parliament increased, as Charles and Buckingham's vision of a glorious campaign against Spain collapsed with an abortive naval expedition to Cadiz in 1625, leading Parliament to demand Buckingham's impeachment. Charles would not sacrifice his dearest friend and dissolved Parliament without any supply being voted. The king therefore attempted to obtain money by alternative means, demanding a forced loan and imprisoning any who refused to pay.

In 1627, Buckingham personally commanded an expedition to free the Protestant Huguenots from French rule at La Rochelle. The expedition was a disaster. Buckingham was blamed and hostility towards him crystallised into the belief that he was the cause of all the ills in the realm. Nevertheless, the duke and the king were determined to plan another expedition, which forced Charles to call a new Parliament in 1628 to vote supply. Desperate for money to finance the war, the king was reluctantly compelled to accept a Petition of Right.

DEATH OF BUCKINGHAM

Buckingham was assassinated by disaffected Puritan John Felton at Portsmouth on 23 August 1628, where he was about to command another naval expedition to La Rochelle. Charles was at nearby Southwick at his morning devotions, when news was brought of his favourite's murder. He received the news impassively, but wept bitterly in the privacy of his own chamber, where for two days he remained in grief-stricken solitude.

Buckingham's death could have been the opportunity for improved relations with Parliament, but this did not happen. New grievances were aired and the king determined to dissolve Parliament. Learning of this intention, a few members physically restrained the Speaker in his seat and passed a set of motions known as 'The Protestation', dealing with religion and the king's collection of customs duties. Once Parliament had been dissolved, the ringleaders were arrested. Parliament would not sit again until 1640.

PERSONAL RULE

The period between the dissolution of Charles's third Parliament in 1629 and his summoning of the Short Parliament in 1640 is known as the 'Personal Rule'. During this period, the king was his own first minister and governed through institutions and officials who were chosen by and answerable to himself. Government was centred on the Privy Council. After Buckingham's assassination, Charles's closest relationship now was with his wife, Henrietta Maria, known as Queen Mary, with whom he had nine children.

Charles I by Daniel Mytens, *c.* 1631. (Author's collection)

Opposite: Charles I and Henrietta Maria dining in public by Gerard Houckgeest, 1635. (Author's collection)

The years of Personal Rule were years of reform and refurbishment. The wars with Spain and France were ended, the '*Book of Orders*', issued in 1631, streamlined poor law administration and the training and equipment of the militia were improved and revenues increased.

Charles's subjects did not appear to be overly concerned that Parliament should not meet and there was nothing illegal in his deciding to rule without summoning Parliament, as this body was traditionally called to provide the monarch with supply; if this was not needed, it was not called. In the reigns of Elizabeth I and James I, there had been long periods when Parliament had not met, such as between 1614 and 1621. There was no increase in levels of public violence, there were fewer sedition trials and England did not slide into anarchy.

A FORMAL AND CULTURED COURT

The court of Charles I was very different from that of his father and was in many ways a reflection of the king himself. Gone were the 'fools and bawds, mimics and catamites' of former days; the court now became the political focus and centre of the king's rule, reflecting his love of order, formality and ceremony, and reflecting his aesthetic sense. Sophisticated, 'temperate, chaste and serious', the familiarity of James I's court was replaced by strict etiquette. However, although more formal and cultured, Charles was aloof, inaccessible, reserved and seriously out of touch with his subjects.

The king built up a royal collection of around 1,700 paintings and sculptures from all over Europe. Rubens's panels for the ceiling of the Banqueting House in Whitehall, celebrating the *Apotheosis of James I,* were installed in 1636–37, while portraits by Anthony van Dyck presented an elegant and devoted royal family. The Masque, a lavish presentation of music, speech and dance, with elaborate costumes, scenery and stage machinery, remained popular and the king and queen frequently took part, to the disapproval of some Puritans.

FAVOURITES AND LOVERS

Although Charles I and Henrietta Maria have usually been regarded as a model of marital devotion, there were rumours during their life-times that even they were not always faithful.

The queen's preference for her favourite, Henry Jermyn, 1st Earl of Saint Albans, was well-known and there was gossip that he was the father of Charles II; this notion was made more credible by Charles's marked dissimilarity to the king. Jermyn's favour continued after the execution of Charles I, and some believed that he was married to the widowed queen, although there is little evidence of this being true.

Jane Whorwood was a Royalist supporter during the Civil War, when she was active in circulating intelligence and smuggling funds. During the king's imprisonment, she was involved in co-ordinating his escape attempts and was a frequent correspondent while he was captive at Carisbrooke Castle on the Isle of Wight, when it seems likely that they conducted a clandestine affair.

THE BEAUTY OF HOLINESS

In the 1630s, the king and Archbishop William Laud embarked upon a renovation of the Church, emphasising their belief that worship should be sacramental and devotional. Altars were positioned at the east end of the sanctuary and surrounded by rails, emphasising the holiness of the area which was set apart for sacramental worship, and organs were installed.

Charles and Laud were confident that what they were doing was within the spectrum of doctrine and practice laid down by the Elizabethan Settlement of

1559, but many Puritans took exception to these changes, even to the extent of sometimes smashing and defacing church furnishings.

Despite the rigidity of the king's religious beliefs, no one was executed for their beliefs during the period 1625–1640, in contrast to all his predecessors; punishments were rare and fewer ministers were deprived or suspended than in most previous decades since the Reformation.

THE BISHOPS' WARS

Charles had left Scotland at the age of four and only visited the land of his birth once, in 1633. Unlike his father, he had little experience or understanding of Scottish politics and was seriously out of touch with his northern kingdom. His interventions in Scottish affairs had provoked hostility, but, most significantly, he determined to bring the Scottish Kirk in line with the English Church, thereby enraging the Scottish Presbyterians.

In October 1636, the king announced the imposition of a new Prayer Book, which was unacceptable to the majority of the population and which provoked riots. In February 1638, a National Covenant was formed, in which the greater parts of influential groups in Scotland bound themselves by a solemn oath to resist the changes, and nine months later the Kirk met and abolished the episcopacy.

Charles I by Anthony van Dyck, *c.* 1635–37. (Author's collection)

Charles attempted to mobilise the militia, but his army was insufficient and he was forced to negotiate. The king accepted a truce at Berwick in the summer of 1639, but the Scots continued to demand that bishops should be removed from the Kirk and that every male should be required to take the Covenant. Charles recalled Thomas Wentworth, recently created Earl of Strafford, from Ireland for advice, who urged him to recall Parliament to obtain money to raise an army.

CONFLICT

Parliament met for the first time in eleven years on 13 April 1640. The members were unfavourable to the king's demands, claiming that the last session had met before their grievances were met, and the Commons demanded the redress of these grievances before they would grant supply. Arminianism, the use of prerogative courts, monopolies, ship money and the collection of customs duties without Parliamentary consent were listed as concerns which must be addressed. Angered by Parliament's attitude, Charles dissolved it after only three weeks.

The king and Strafford sought ways to raise sufficient money to put down the Scottish revolt, but the royal forces were routed at the Battle of Newburn and Charles was forced to abandon Newcastle and its coalfields to the Scots. The king agreed to another truce in October, conceding to pay the Scots £850 a day until peace terms were agreed. With winter approaching and the Scots in control of London's coal supply, but with insufficient funds to fulfil the financial obligations of the truce, Charles was in an impossible position; his only option was to recall Parliament.

ESCALATION

When Charles I called the Long Parliament in November 1640, none would have recognised or feared that civil war was imminent. Led by the Earl of Bedford in the Lords and John Pym in the Commons, the vast majority of MPs were united in their determination to dismantle everything which had enabled the king to rule without Parliament. They demanded that Charles agree to call Parliament regularly and, under the Triennial Act, Charles reluctantly agreed that Parliament should meet at least every three years and for a minimum of fifty days. Parliament's position was strengthened further by an Act preventing the dissolution of Parliament without its own consent.

Strafford and Laud were impeached and the former was executed on Tower Hill in May 1641, despite the king's pleas that his life be spared. Laud was imprisoned, but followed Strafford to the block four years later. Freed from the threat of dissolution, Parliament abolished the prerogative courts of Star Chamber and High Commission and went on to declare all Charles's financial devices illegal, including ship money, enforced knighthoods and the collection of tonnage and poundage without Parliamentary consent. Pym's Ten Propositions of June 1641, which called for the king to submit his choice of ministers to Parliament for their approval, was viewed with concern by some MPs as dangerously radical and unlikely to be acceptable to the king.

By the summer of 1641, the situation between the king and Parliament had reached a stalemate. However, exaggerated reports of atrocities by Irish Catholics upon Protestant settlers, as well as rumours that an Irish army had landed in England with the king's consent, caused widespread fear and panic.

'I SEE THE BIRDS HAVE FLOWN'

Pym and others proposed that Parliament should maintain control of the army, which was regarded as an insulting infringement of the royal prerogative by an increasing number of MPs. The Grand Remonstrance introduced by Pym on 22 November, followed by a Militia Bill, caused further outrage and many MPs now rallied to the king.

Believing that Pym was intending to impeach the queen, the king ordered the Lords to begin impeachment proceedings against five MPs, including Pym and Hampden. When the Lords declined to act, Charles set off from Whitehall Palace

St William's College, York, which housed the Royal printing presses during the Civil War. (Courtesy of the Chapter of York)

with an armed retinue to make the arrest in person, only to find that they had been warned and had escaped. Six days later, fearing for the safety of his family, Charles left London for Hampton Court and sent the queen to safety in France. In February, the court was moved to York.

THE FIRST CIVIL WAR

The Civil War commenced on 22 August 1642, when King Charles raised his standard at Nottingham, although at this stage there was little desire for hostilities on either side. The king moved to Shrewsbury, accompanied by his nephew Prince Rupert, who was the son of his sister Elizabeth, and marched towards London. He was intercepted at Edgehill, Warwickshire, on 23 October, where his army was engaged in battle by Parliamentary forces commanded by the Earl of Essex. Charles continued his advance on London but was blocked by Essex's forces on the capital's outskirts and retreated to Oxford, which became his headquarters for the rest of the war.

During the spring and summer of 1643, the king enjoyed his greatest successes, with victories at Adwalton Moor in Yorkshire and Lansdown in Somerset and the capture of Bristol.

However, the 'Royalist summer' came to an end in the early autumn of 1643, when Essex's army forced the king to raise the siege of Gloucester, followed by a

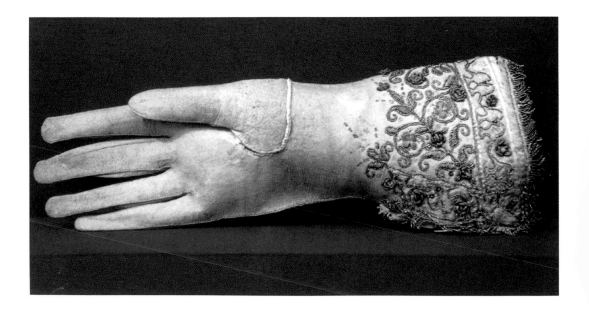

stalemate at the First Battle of Newbury and a victory for the Parliamentarians at the Battle of Winceby.

Parliament offered concessions to the Scots in return for aid and assistance, and in January 1644 a well-disciplined army of 20,000 troops crossed over the border, laying siege to Newcastle. Shortly afterwards, Charles confirmed the Cessation Treaty with the Irish rebels in order to bring his troops home to England. This action was used as propaganda by Parliament, which provoked fear by claiming that the king was employing Irish Catholics to suppress his Protestant subjects.

Forces under Sir Thomas Fairfax caught and destroyed the Irish army which had landed in Cheshire, and the Royalist army was defeated at Cheriton in Hampshire. In 1644, Charles lost control of the north of England when the Royalists were defeated by the combined armies of Parliament and the Scots at the Battle of Marston Moor, the bloodiest battle of the Civil War.

The Battle of Lostwithiel in Cornwall, the last major victory for the Royalists, was followed by the Second Battle of Newbury in October 1644, which resulted in a tactical victory for Parliament.

THE NEW MODEL ARMY

Divisions between the peace party and the war party, and between Oliver Cromwell and the Earl of Manchester, who desired a negotiated peace with the

Previous page: Glove of Queen Henrietta Maria. (Courtesy of the Lords Feoffees and Assistants of the Manor of Bridlington)

Right: Musket balls from the Battle of Marston Moor, 2 July 1644. (Author's collection)

king, led to the Self-Denying Ordinance of January 1645, which excluded any Members of Parliament from holding positions of military command. Manchester and Essex were relieved of their posts but Cromwell was exempted. This was followed by the creation of one unified army, known as the New Model Army, under the command of Sir Thomas Fairfax, which inflicted a fatal blow to the king's forces at the Battle of Naseby in June 1645.

Another Parliamentary victory at Langport, Somerset, witnessed the beginning of the end for the king. In the spring of 1646, the New Model Army laid siege to Oxford. Charles evaded capture, but surrendered to the Scots at Newark, hoping that he could negotiate better terms with them than with Parliament.

BY THE SWORD DIVIDED

The pain experienced by many families and friends who fought on opposing sides in the Civil War is encapsulated in the following letter from Susan, Countess of Denbigh. After the death of her Royalist husband in battle, she begs her son, Basil Feilding, to leave the Parliamentarians and return to the king who had done so much for their family.

I beg of you my first born son to give me the comfort of that son I do so dearly love, that satisfaction which you owe me now, which is to leave those that murdered your dear father, for what can it be called, but so? Which when he received his death wounds but with the saying that he was for the King, there was no mercy for his grey hairs, but wounds and shots; a horror to me to think of.

O my dear Jesus, put it into my son's heart to leave that merciless way that was the death of his father, for now I think of it with horror, before with sorrow ... The last words your dear father spoke of you was to desire God to forgive you and to touch your heart ... I do believe that you are not so much respected by that party as you think you are, for they do many things and make many offers to save themselves ...

So with my blessing, I take my leave,

Your loving mother, Susan Denbigh.

Henrietta Maria by Anthony van Dyck, *c.* 1638. (Author's collection)

THE SEARCH FOR A SETTLEMENT

Although Charles had been defeated, few Parliamentarians could envisage a settlement without the agreement and co-operation of the king. In January 1647, the Scots handed Charles over to Parliament. When the Commons voted to disband the New Model Army foot regiments, they seized control of the king, issued a declaration demanding settlement of arrears in pay, a purge of their Parliamentary opponents and new elections, and confirmed their opposition to Presbyterianism. While discussions and debates divided his opponents, the king secretly negotiated with the Scots.

In December 1647, Charles briefly escaped and secured a deal with the Scots, known as the 'Engagement', in which he promised to introduce Presbyterianism into England and suppress all non-conformists. In return, the Scots promised the king an army to restore him to his throne.

THE SECOND CIVIL WAR

In April 1648, an outbreak of rebellions in Essex, Kent and South Wales was dealt with by the army. In July, the Scots invaded, but in the following month their forces were defeated by Cromwell at Preston, Lancashire. A majority within

Parliament still desired a settlement with the king and the Commons voted to continue negotiations, but, in December 1648, in an action known as 'Pride's Purge', MPs at Westminster found their way barred by a large force, under Colonel Thomas Pride. Half of the MPs who were eligible to sit in the Commons were barred and forty-five were arrested. The remaining MPs were known as 'the Rump', although less than half were prepared to be involved in the king's trial.

'WE WILL CUT OFF HIS HEAD WITH THE CROWN UPON IT': TRIAL AND EXECUTION

On 1 January 1649, the Rump passed an ordinance to bring the king to trial. Despite the Lords' rejection of the ordinance, they passed a further measure to establish a special High Court of Justice and proceeded without the Lords' support. Several prominent Parliamentarians refused to serve and Fairfax, wishing to have no part in regicide, attended only once.

The king's trial lasted from 20 to 27 January. The outcome was already decided and Charles was fully aware that he would be declared guilty. He refused to respond to any of the accusations, claiming, in a voice which retained no traces of

Charles I on his way to his execution. From the painting by Ernest Croft. (Author's collection)

Cromwell before the Coffin of Charles I by Paul Delaroche, 1831. This painting is based on the story that after the execution Cromwell paid a private visit to St James's Palace and, looking down on the dead king in his open coffin, was heard to murmur, 'Cruel necessity.' (Author's collection)

his former speech impediment, that the court had no legal authority to try him. It was his finest hour. The king's calm and dignified behaviour throughout his trial impressed even those who had been exasperated by his intransigence.

Charles I was condemned to death and was executed outside his own Banqueting House at Whitehall on Tuesday 30 January 1649, famously wearing two shirts so that he would not shiver and be thought afraid on a day so cold that the Thames had frozen over.

The king's death was deeply troubling to many of his people. Monarchs had died violently in wars and coups, but this was particularly shocking because the king had been tried like a common felon and executed by a small minority of his own people.

3
THE REPUBLIC
1649–1660

CHALLENGES FOR THE NEW REGIME

The execution of King Charles I in January 1649 provoked a wave of shock and revulsion; the loud groan that rose from the crowd as the axe severed the king's head from his shoulders symbolised the horror and outrage felt by the majority of Charles's subjects. There had been little support for regicide from either the people or from Parliament and there were anti-English demonstrations abroad.

The Rump was the remnant of Parliament after Colonel Pride purged the Long Parliament in December 1648 of those members hostile to the Grandees' intention to put the king on trial; it was a link with the old constitution and regarded as an interim government. Supporters of the new regime, who held differing views, faced the task of redefining and establishing a workable constitution without a monarchy. The army demanded a greater social transformation to accompany the political changes, while the Rump was concerned in calming conservative fears of social disorder and anarchy, compounded by radical sects such as the Ranters.

Within weeks the regime, which was only supported by a minority of the population, faced threats from Royalists abroad and Levellers at home. On 17 March 1649, the Rump passed an Act abolishing the office of king and abolished the House of Lords, which had refused to support the proceedings against Charles I. Radicals who had initially supported the Rump soon discovered that there were to be no further reforms, and demands that the Rump be dissolved and replaced by a Parliament elected by universal male suffrage was ignored, with the Rump ordering the suppression of the Levellers.

THE THIRD CIVIL WAR

The Rump's greatest concern was how to deal with the situation in Ireland, where Royalist supporters of Charles II had formed an alliance with the Irish Confederates, causing fears that it could be used as a base for invasion. Cromwell was sent with a large force to deal with the threat, which he did with great brutality. In 1650 he was recalled to deal with the threat from the Scots, who, angered at the execution of the king, had allied themselves with his son, Charles II. Cromwell, now the commander of the army after the resignation of Sir Thomas Fairfax, defeated the Royalist forces at Dunbar and achieved a decisive victory over Charles II at Worcester in September 1651.

A BALANCING ACT

The Rump attempted to regain the support of the more conservative members by avoiding any radical reform, but this had to be balanced with the demands of the army, on whose support the Rump was dependent. The situation was exacerbated by financial difficulties. The Rump dared not disband the army, which was costly to maintain, and by 1653 the Rump faced a short-fall of £700,000, despite taxes being raised.

The breakdown of the National Church, which had followed the abolition of bishops, caused great disquiet and the teachings of religious sects such as the Quakers and Ranters were perceived as a threat to social hierarchy. Therefore, although the Rump repealed the Act which made church attendance compulsory,

MAY DAY CELEBRATIONS

Attempts at discouraging the populace from enjoying the traditional celebrations on May Day were unpopular with many and met with limited success, much to the disapproval of one Puritan observer:

Monday 1 May 1654
This day was more observed by people going a-maying than for divers years past; and indeed, much sin committed by wicked meetings with fiddlers, drunkenness, ribaldry and the like; great resort came to Hyde Park, many hundreds of coaches and gallants in sport, but most shameful, powdered-hair men and painted and spotted women. Some men played with a silver ball and some took other recreation. But his Highness the Lord Protector went not hither, nor any of the lords of the Commonwealth, but were busy about the great affairs of the Commonwealth.

it did not meet the demands of the army and independents by agreeing to full religious toleration.

Fear of political and social instability led to the reintroduction of censorship under the direction of John Milton, followed by the Blasphemy Act and the introduction of the Adultery Act in 1650. Other changes were introduced, and all court proceedings were now conducted in English rather than in Old French or Latin.

The Rump was more successful in foreign affairs, with the introduction of the Navigation Act in October 1651. War with the Dutch followed in 1652, in which the English fleet, under the command of Robert Blake, defeated the Dutch in several engagements. Large amounts of Dutch shipping were seized and, by the end of the following year, the United Provinces opened negotiations to end the war.

THE DISSOLUTION OF THE RUMP AND THE PARLIAMENT OF SAINTS

By September 1651, the Rump had agreed to its own dissolution, although it had reserved the right to decide on what and who should succeed it. Cromwell had by now lost patience. He entered the House of Commons in April 1653, accompanied by troops, and forcibly ended their sitting. Ironically, the army that Parliament had created to protect its liberties had turned upon its creator and now the rule of the Commonwealth was in in its hands and that of its commander-in-chief, Oliver Cromwell. Contemporaries were divided regarding the dissolution of the Rump and uncertain as to Cromwell's motives, as well as what would fill the political vacuum.

A new governmental body was created, named the Parliament of Saints and nick-named 'The Barebones Parliament' by Royalist propagandists. It consisted of 140 members, who were selected by the army's council of officers. The majority were conservative landowners of gentry background, but some sought a reform of the law based on principles of the Old Testament, with the abolition of tithes and holders of impropriated tithes. However, such reforms would have alienated those groups on whom Cromwell depended for support. The moderates within the assembly met early on the morning of 12 December and voted the Parliament's dissolution before the arrival of the more radical members. The radicals' determination to hold a session led to their dispersal from the House of Commons by armed troops.

THE PROTECTORATE

With the failure of the Parliament of Saints, Cromwell accepted the suggestion of General John Lambert in 1653 of a written form of constitution, known as the Instrument of Government, which laid down the powers and rights of the executive and legislature. These included that executive power was to be held by a Lord Protector, who would be Cromwell, with the assistance of a Council of State. Parliament was to be called at least once every three years and could not be dissolved without its own consent.

Cromwell was formally installed as Lord Protector at Westminster Hall on 16 December 1653 and in the following April he moved into Whitehall Palace,

Oliver Cromwell, Lord Protector, unknown artist, *c.* 1650. (Courtesy of Rijksmuseum, Amsterdam)

the former residence of Charles I. His decision to accept the office of Protector alienated many republicans and religious radicals, who regarded it as a betrayal of the principles for which the Civil War had been fought.

Cromwell ruled directly by ordinance (decree) until the first Protectorate Parliament met in September 1654.

When some of his opponents attacked the division of powers outlined in the Instrument, Cromwell responded by ordering troops to surround the House of Commons and demanding that the Instrument be recognised, provoking a walk-out by a hundred members. Those opponents who remained continued to call for limitations on Cromwell's powers, both in Parliamentary control over the militia and the appointments to the Council of State, and to demand changes to the Instrument's provision for religious toleration. Cromwell dissolved Parliament in January 1655 and ruled by ordinance.

THE MAJOR-GENERALS

A Royalist rising in Wiltshire early in 1655 resulted in the imposition of direct military rule of the country, dividing it into eleven districts, each of which was under the control of a major-general. These were given authority to maintain internal security and suppress immorality, aided by a new militia which was paid by a ten percent tax on the estates of known Royalists. The effectiveness of the scheme varied from area to area, with alehouses being closed and traditional entertainments such as stage-plays, cock-fighting and horse-racing being suppressed. Such impositions were resented, and were regarded as undermining the position and role of the gentry.

THE SECOND PROTECTORATE PARLIAMENT

When war with Spain broke out in 1656, like Charles I in 1640, Cromwell was reluctantly compelled to recall Parliament, which reassembled in September 1656. Over a hundred MPs who were critical of the regime were excluded, leading to the withdrawal of a further sixty in protest. The remainder of Parliament voted £400,000 for the Spanish war, but expressed concern over the policy of religious toleration, sentencing the Quaker James Naylor to death for having claimed to be Christ. Although Cromwell intervened and his life was spared, Naylor was brutally punished. Cromwell found that like his predecessors, James I and Charles I, he was compelled to agree to concessions in order to ensure supply.

KING OLIVER?

A set of proposals, known as the Humble Petition and Advice, were put forward by Parliament in 1657, with the most significant proposal being that Cromwell should accept the throne. He eventually declined, probably because the army opposed the idea, as did his closest associates; Clarendon claimed that there was a plot to kill him if he accepted the crown. However, the rest of the amendments were accepted, which included that the Protector should be able to appoint his own successor, that Parliament would consist of two houses (the second of which would consist of members nominated by the Protector), that no members elected to the Commons could be excluded from it and that a Confession of Faith was to be agreed by the Protector and Parliament, which none could criticise without being punished.

Cromwell was reinstalled as Lord Protector on 26 June 1657, with many of the trappings of royalty, wearing a robe of purple velvet lined with ermine and carrying

WARTS AND ALL

Many remedies were used to remove unsightly warts.

The use of radishes shredded into a pewter dish, salted, covered, violently shaken and then rubbed on the wart three times a day was believed to be effective. Other cures recommended that a slice of potato be tied to the wart or stone lime placed in water, boiled then mixed with barrel soap, spread on a cloth and applied. Less painful was to carve one's initials in the bark of an ash tree and as the bark healed, so would the wart.

Warts were considered to be lucky by some, especially hairy ones. Oliver Cromwell had a great wart on his chin, which signified wealth, a good digestion and eloquence in speech. The two warts on the right side of his forehead again signified wealth. Had they been on the left side, it would have signified poverty.

It is unlikely that the Lord Protector would have subscribed to such superstitions. However, his famous instructions to the painter Sir Peter Lely to 'paint my picture truly like me, and not flatter me at all; but remark all these roughnesses, pimples, warts and everything as you see me, otherwise I will never pay a farthing for it', may not be factual.

a golden sceptre. He took an adapted form of the royal coronation oath and left Westminster Hall in a coach of state to cries of 'God save the Lord Protector'. King in all but name, Cromwell was usually addressed as 'your Highness' and had been rewarding his loyal followers with knighthoods since 1656.

Hopes for more harmonious relations with Parliament were dashed during Parliament's second session in January 1658. Both the constitution and Cromwell's increased powers were attacked and a petition circulating in London calling for the abolition of the second chamber and the Protectorate provoked Cromwell into once more dissolving Parliament.

RELIGIOUS POLICY

Cromwell was deeply opposed to any form of religious control and favoured a broad religious tolerance, although this excluded Catholics and sects which were regarded as subversive, such as Ranters and Quakers. However, this approach occasioned anger from both sides of the religious divide; conservatives feared anarchy, while the members of the sects were angered that they were denied the freedom they demanded.

Two ordinances were issued in 1654. A central commission, later known as 'Triers', was established to ensure that all new clergymen were orthodox, godly men. Another commission, later known as 'Ejectors', dealt with clergy already in post who were regarded as inadequate in their personal and religious lives. Under Cromwell's government, there was a far greater degree of religious freedom than at any other period in seventeenth-century England.

FOREIGN POLICY

Cromwell achieved his greatest success in the field of foreign policy. During the Lord Protector's rule, England improved its international standing and trade through a series of treaties and enjoyed an expansion of influence and power. Peace was maintained with the Dutch, and treaties with Sweden and Denmark opened the Baltic to English merchants. Cromwell was active in creating a European-wide Protestant alliance and mediated between the Dutch and Swedes over trading conflicts. Despite being a devout Protestant, Cromwell's primary concern was England's foreign interests and he was not averse to allying with Catholic France if he thought it would best serve the country's interests. An English expedition against Spanish colonies in the Caribbean captured Jamaica,

Death Mask of Oliver Cromwell,
taken from the original cast in the
British Museum. (P. J. Womack.
Reproduced with permission of Bradford
Metropolitan District Council, Bradford
Museums and Galleries)

which was a valuable asset in the future. In October 1655, war broke out with Spain, which saw significant English successes and ensured England's dominance of the seas.

THE COLLAPSE OF THE REPUBLIC

Oliver Cromwell died on 3 September 1658 at the age of fifty-nine, probably from a recurrence of malaria. He was buried in Westminster Abbey with an elaborate funeral service based upon that of King James I. Within eight months, the Protectorate had disintegrated. History has been greatly divided over Cromwell, as were his contemporaries; to some he is a champion of Parliamentary democracy, to others a power-hungry hypocrite.

The succession of Cromwell's son Richard was peaceful and unopposed. Nicknamed 'Tumbledown Dick', Richard Cromwell had served in the Parliamentary army during the Civil War but lacked his father's military skill and his indomitable personality. Intelligent and diligent, he had little experience of government and little ambition, and he was unable to command the same degree of loyalty and authority over the army as had his father. Richard supported proposals that the political activities of the army and the extent of religious toleration should be restricted. The army responded swiftly and the day after Parliament had voted on the proposals, Richard was forced to dissolve it and then abdicate. The Protectorate was over.

ANARCHY

The Rump was recalled, but its declaration that all Acts and ordinances passed since its dissolution in 1653 were illegal and its attempt to arrest General Lambert led to its being once again forcibly dissolved. The army now assumed military rule and a Committee of Safety was established by the Council of Officers. The country slipped into political anarchy and, amid rumours of a Quaker rising, General George Monck, commander of the army in Scotland, declared his support for the Rump and civilian government.

On 1 January 1660, Monck crossed the river Tweed into England with 10,000 troops, vowing that he would deliver the realm from 'the intolerable slavery of sword government'. The Committee of Safety authorised Lambert to raise a force in Yorkshire to resist him. However, morale and the will to fight had collapsed and the army slipped away as Monck approached. The Rump was restored once more, and, as Monck moved south, he was inundated with petitions for a free Parliament and for the return of the monarchy by a population desperate for stability.

ORDER RESTORED

In February 1660, Monck recalled the MPs who had been excluded in 1648, on condition that they dissolve Parliament and call free elections. In the meantime, he was involved in secret negotiations with Charles II, leading to the Declaration of Breda, on 4 April. Chiefly drafted by Charles's main advisor, Sir Edward Hyde, an amnesty was declared for all except those who had been involved in the trial and death of his father. Freedom of religion would be granted to all, provided they did not threaten the peace of the realm. All arrears of pay would be settled with the officers and soldiers under Monck's command, and issues of lands lost by Royalists were to be decided by Parliament.

On May I 1660, Parliament voted for a restoration of the traditional form of government 'by King, Lords, and Commons'. On 29 May, Charles II entered London amid scenes of joy.

4

CHARLES II
1660–1685

AN ENGLISH PRINCE

As Venus, the planet of love, shone brightly in the early morning sky on 29 May 1630, Queen Henrietta Maria, wife to Charles I, went into labour at St James's Palace. Eight gruelling hours later she gave birth to her first surviving child, a strong, lusty son who was named Charles. From his Italian maternal grandmother, the prince inherited the thick, lustrous black hair and olive skin that earned him the name 'Black Boy', and he would grow to tower over his tiny parents.

Church bells pealed and bonfires were lit to celebrate the arrival of an heir to the throne, who was joined the next year by the Princess Royal, Mary. James was born in 1633, followed by Elizabeth, Anne and Henry. At the age of eight, Charles was given his own court at Richmond. He was entrusted to the care of William Cavendish, Earl of Newcastle, a courteous and kindly nobleman whose influence on the developing prince was more profound than that of his parents, whom he saw infrequently.

WAR

The beginning of the end of Charles's life of security and privilege came on 22 August 1642, when, at the age of twelve, he stood by his father the king as the royal standard was raised at Nottingham. For the prince and his younger brother James, the war was initially a time of excitement when they believed the Royalists would gain an early victory secured by their dashing young cousin, Prince Rupert. Both young princes witnessed the first battle of the war at Edgehill, where a cannonball narrowly missed Charles. However, the longed-for victory eluded the king and, to encourage his troops, he sent his eldest son to Bristol early in 1645, appointing him as General of the Western army.

By the summer, the Parliamentarians had won another resounding victory at Naseby and shortly afterwards the king urged Charles to prepare his escape. The prince and his advisers retreated before the advancing enemy troops, seeking refuge

Charles II when Prince of Wales
by Nicholas Thach. (Courtesy of
Rijksmuseum, Amsterdam)

at Pendennis Castle in Cornwall, where Charles was informed of the final Royalist
defeat at Torrington. On 2 March 1646, Charles reluctantly slipped away on board
the *Phoenix* for the Scillies, where he stayed for six weeks, desperately short of
money, food and clothing. It was a far cry from his former life of pampered luxury.

EXILE

On 16 April, Charles embarked for Jersey, which was still loyal to the king,
later joining his mother in France. Denied any political role and largely ignored
at the court of his eight year-old cousin, Louis XIV, and his powerful chief
minister, Cardinal Mazarin, Charles spent his time studying mathematics with
Thomas Hobbes, indulging his interest in scientific experiments and his interest
in the fairer sex together with his old playmate, George Villiers, 2nd Duke of
Buckingham.

In the summer of 1648, a Parliamentary fleet surrendered to the Royalists and,
eager for action, Charles joined it in Holland, assuming nominal command; this
was to the annoyance of his brother James, Duke of York, who had recently escaped

from England and was Lord High Admiral. Charles's ambition to engage the enemy fleet, commanded by the Earl of Warwick, was thwarted and he was forced to return to Holland. At The Hague, Charles began a passionate affair with Lucy Walter, a young English refugee, who bore him a son, named James, in April 1649.

A KING WITHOUT A THRONE

The eagerly awaited news from England was grim. When Charles heard that his father was to be tried for his life, he made desperate attempts to save him, including sending a letter to Parliament, offering any terms if the king's life were spared. His pleas were ignored, and Charles only learned the truth when his chaplain addressed him as 'Your Majesty'. The new king fled weeping to his chamber.

The crowned heads of Europe, shocked by the regicide of an anointed monarch, recognised the prince as Charles II, and Charles made plans to retake his throne. His first choice of leading a Catholic army in Ireland was destroyed by Cromwell's ruthless campaign in that country and so he turned to the Scots. Charles was compelled to swear solemn oaths to reform his life, dismissing his companions and agreeing to the death of his most prominent Scottish supporter, the Earl of Montrose. He also vowed to impose the Presbyterian faith in England and Ireland – vows which he had no intention of keeping.

Charles landed in Scotland in the summer of 1650. He was allowed no part or say in the organising of the army and, as Cromwell's crack troops marched into Scotland, the Scots leaders dismissed 3,000 of their best troops, branding them as 'malignants' and replacing them with ministers' sons and others who were inexperienced in warfare. It was, inevitably, a slaughter. Charles attempted to escape from the Scots, but was overtaken and returned to his captors.

Charles was crowned on 1 January 1651 and, although his coronation was a day of pomp and pageant, two days were designated as days of national repentance and humiliation for the sins of the royal family. As he listened wearily to the interminable catalogue of sins which he must acknowledge, he murmured, 'I think I must repent, too, that ever I was born.'

WORCESTER

Throughout the spring and summer of 1651, a new army was raised and, with Charles at its head, marched into England. He had been convinced that he would be joined by thousands of loyal subjects, but few followed him; there was little enthusiasm for an army of Scots and all were aware of the gruesome fate which awaited traitors. As Charles reached Worcester, Parliamentary troops were already waiting; his forces were decisively beaten and he himself narrowly avoided capture. Realising that his best chance now lay in leaving the remnants of his army, he and a few companions slipped away.

'A TALL BLACK MAN UPWARDS OF TWO YARDS HIGH'

In the following weeks, Charles was a fugitive with a price on his head. He succeeded in eluding his pursuers with the help of a royal network and by his wits and charm, famously hiding in an oak tree and in a priest hole belonging to a local Catholic family. Disguised by a blackened face and shorn hair, Charles travelled as Will Jackson, servant to a colonel's daughter, Jane Lane, journeying to the south coast. Many guessed his identity, but none betrayed him. He finally gained a passage in a collier brig from Shoreham in Sussex to Normandy.

For the next nine years Charles wandered from country to country and court to court, vainly seeking support. These years of exile affected him profoundly and he learnt the art of political manoeuvre and intrigue. He developed a deep mistrust of both friends and enemies, believing that few loved him for himself, and developed a strong sense of political survival and capacity for intrigue; these were traits which were evident throughout his reign.

THE RETURN OF THE KING

In 1658 Oliver Cromwell died, but his successor, his son Richard, had neither the ability nor the experience to govern. Within eight months, the Protectorate had disintegrated. In March 1660, George Monck, a former royalist who commanded the Parliamentary troops in Scotland, dispatched Sir John Grenville to Charles's court. On Monck's advice, Charles removed himself from the Catholic Spanish dominions and took up residence in Breda, where he was joined by hundreds of Royalists. Monck marched from Scotland, declaring his intention to call a Free Parliament. The Declaration of Breda, masterminded by Edward Hyde, in which Charles pardoned his enemies and swore to uphold the Anglican Church while granting 'liberty to tender consciences', was received by Parliament with joy and relief.

Shortly afterwards, preparations were underway for Charles's return to England. The young king boarded the flagship *The Naseby*, tactfully renamed *The Royal Charles*, and set sail at last for his kingdom.

Restoration Procession at Cheapside
by William Hogarth, *c.* 1745.
(Courtesy of Yale Center for British
Art, Paul Mellon Fund)

THE PRETTIEST WOMAN IN THE WHOLE HOUSE

In 1660, the theatres were reopened after eighteen years and on 18 August Samuel Pepys saw his first play at the Cockpit Theatre in Drury Lane; it was a tragicomedy by John Fletcher entitled *The Loyal Subject*.

The twenty-year-old actor Edward Kynaston played the main female lead and Pepys found him 'the loveliest lady that I ever saw in my life'. Kynaston went onto achieve fame, acting both male and female roles, and was rumoured to be the lover of George Villiers, 2nd Duke of Buckingham.

However, a royal warrant was issued in 1662, declaring that all female roles should be played only by female actresses and in January 1661 Pepys noted that he had seen a woman act for the first time ever in *The Beggar's Bush* at the Theatre Royal.

Margaret Hughes may have been the first professional actress in England, appearing as Desdemona in Shakespeare's *Othello* on 8 December 1660. She had several influential lovers, notably Charles II and Prince Rupert, whose daughter she bore.

On St George's Day, 23 April 1661, the king was crowned Charles II. Clever and witty, with a cynicism engendered by his wandering youth, Charles was restless, easily bored and frequently sentimental and generous. He loved to be entertained and to be made to laugh, and enjoyed scandalous tales. The new king married Catherine of Braganza, daughter of the King of Portugal, on 21 May at Portsmouth.

EARLY REIGN

Those still living who had actually taken part in the trial and execution of the king's father were brought to trial and executed. Unlike the public, who cheered at the grisly spectacle, Charles derived little pleasure from their deaths, commenting that 'I must confess that I am weary of hanging, except upon new offences'. On the anniversary of Charles I's execution, the bodies of Cromwell, Bradshaw and Ireton were exhumed and hung in chains, with their heads stuck on poles over Westminster Hall. The army was paid off and granted immunity from prosecution.

The Restoration Court was extravagant, hedonistic and thought to be decadent and immoral by some observers, such as Pepys, himself no saint, who commented on 'the lewdness and beggary ... ' However, the king included his passion for science in his pleasurable pursuits, which led to the establishment of the Royal Society and the Royal Observatory in Greenwich.

THE CLARENDON CODE

The Convention Parliament, which had produced a financial settlement that provided the king with revenue from taxation in return for the abolition of his feudal and prerogative powers, was dissolved at the end of 1660 and replaced the following year by the Cavalier Parliament. This restored the king's control over the militia, and replaced the Triennial Act of 1641 with a weaker act which made no provision to call MPs if the king failed to do so.

Censorship was restored in the Licensing Act of 1662, and Parliament brought a change in the religious settlement. The Anglican Church, with its bishops and Prayer Book, was the Church of England, and the Corporation Act stated that only those who took Anglican Communion could be elected to municipal corporations. The Act of Uniformity followed in May 1662, which resulted in most Presbyterians joining with the Baptists, Congregationalists and Quakers, as nonconformists or Protestant dissenters.

Despite the king's sympathy towards the nonconformists, harsh persecutions followed, initiating an attack on Puritan dissenters. Known as the Clarendon Code after Edward Hyde, Earl of Clarendon, who was the king's chief advisor, it included a Conventicle (meeting) Act, which made it illegal for more than five persons not of the same household to meet for religious worship; in a similar vein, the Five Mile Act made it illegal for nonconformist ministers to come within five miles of any city, borough or parish where they had served.

PLAGUE AND FIRE

On a scorchingly hot day in June 1665, Samuel Pepys noted in his diary that he saw a red cross marked on three doors in Drury Lane; the Plague had returned to filthy, overcrowded London. In the first week, there were over a hundred deaths; by the following week the total had risen to over 700 and by September there were 1,000 deaths a day.

Below left: The Great Fire of London with Ludgate and Old St Paul's, unknown artist, *c.* 1670. (Courtesy of Yale Center for British Art, Paul Mellon Fund)

Below right: A physician wearing a seventeenth-century plague preventive costume. (Courtesy of Wellcome Library, London)

TWO TREATMENTS FOR THE PLAGUE

Plague Water:

Take rosemary, red balm, burrage, angelica, carduus, celandine, aragon, feathfew, wormwood, pennyroyal, elecampane, roots, mugwort, bural, tormentil, egrimony, sage, sorrel, of each of these one handful, weighed weight for weight, put all these in an earthen pot, with four quarts of white wine, cover them close and let them stand eight or nine days in a cool cellar, then distil it in a glass still.

Hannah Woolley, *The Queen-like Closet*, 1684

If you be infected with the plague, and feel the assured signs thereof, as pain in the head, drought, burning, weakness of stomach and such like: then you shall take a drachm of the best mithridate and dissolve it in three or four spoonful of dragon-water and immediately drink it off. And then with hot cloths or bricks, made extreme hot and laid to the soles of your feet, after you have been kept in woollen cloths, compel the sick party to sweat, which if he do, keep him moderately therein till the sore begin to rise; then to the same apply a live pigeon cut in two parts, or else a plaster made of the yolk of an egg, honey, herb of grace chopped exceeding small, and wheat flour, which in very small space will not only ripen, but also break the same without any other incision; then after it hath run a day or two, you shall apply a plaster of meliot unto it until it be whole.

Gervase Markham, *The English Hus-wife*, 1615

The Mayor of London immediately ordered emergency measures – watchmen guarded infected houses to keep the inhabitants inside, bodies were heaped into huge pits and buried, dogs were killed, shops, taverns and theatres were closed and a nine o'clock curfew was imposed.

Many fled the city, including the king and court, and dense, black clouds from bonfires, lit in an attempt to purify the air, billowed over the corpse-littered, deserted streets.

More horrors were to follow. Retiring to his bed in Seething Lane in the early hours of Sunday 2 September 1666, Pepys noted a glow over the City. When he woke he was concerned to see the blaze still raging and upon hurrying to the City he found the fire out of control. Pepys rushed to Whitehall to inform the king of the crisis. The fire had begun at a bakery in Pudding Lane, near London Bridge, and burned for four days and nights, destroying eighty per cent of the Old City.

Conspiracy theories abounded, with Roman Catholics or foreigners being blamed. A new London arose from the smouldering ashes, with wider streets and brick houses replacing the former rat-infested dwellings.

THE SECOND DUTCH WAR

In 1665, hostilities with the Dutch were resumed, with a naval victory off Lowestoft in June, but Clarendon was made the scapegoat for an unexpected attack on the naval base at Chatham and was impeached, fleeing to France where he died in 1674.

The Cabal, so named after the initials of the chief members – Clifford, Arlington, Buckingham, Ashley and Lauderdale – dominated the government. However, they were not the only ministers and Charles himself directed royal policy.

In January 1668, the king signed a treaty with the United Provinces and Sweden. Two years later, an alliance with France, Europe's foremost Catholic power, was concluded at Dover. It committed England to make war against the Dutch with France and promised that Charles would receive £225,000 a year for the duration of the war. A secret clause also committed Charles to convert to Roman Catholicism and for Louis to pay him £150,000 and provide 6,000 troops.

THE DECLARATION OF INDULGENCE

Suspicion and distrust surrounding the alliance with France was increased by the king's Declaration of Indulgence in March 1672, which suspended parts of the Uniformity Act, allowing Catholics to worship in private and permitting dissenting Protestants to apply for a licence to worship in public. There were fears that this would lead to a plan to destroy Protestantism and, when the Commons attacked the Declaration, Charles was forced to back down and reconfirm the main provisions of the Clarendon Code in a Test Act, which required holders of public office to deny the Catholic doctrine of Transubstantiation.

The king's position was weakened by the failure of the Dutch war and, faced with massive debts from the wars and Parliamentary hostility to providing further supply, Charles was forced to make peace with the Dutch in February 1674.

Further damage was caused by the conversion to Roman Catholicism of the king's heir, his brother James, Duke of York, in 1673. Recognising the need to abandon his pro-Catholic policies, Charles forged an alliance with the Church party, negotiated by the new Treasurer, Thomas Osborne, Lord Danby, who built up support in Parliament by combining a pro-Dutch foreign policy and a renewed persecution of Catholics and Dissenters. Danby arranged a marriage between the king's niece, Mary, and the Dutch Prince, William of Orange, in 1677.

THE POPISH PLOT

In August 1678 Titus Oates, an expelled naval chaplain who had led a colourful and chequered career, approached the London magistrate, Sir Edmund Berry Godfrey, with a story of a plot organised by the Jesuits and the French to murder the king and replace him on the throne by his Catholic brother James. The story lacked credibility and Oates even more so. However, the plot seemed more believable when, shortly afterwards, Godfrey was found dead and one of the first names Oates had given, Edward Coleman, a former secretary to the Catholic Duke of York, was found to be in communication with the French.

THE EXCLUSION CRISIS

In 1678, new elections produced a majority of opposition MPs who forced the king to accept a new Privy Council, chosen by Parliament, followed with a bill to exclude James from the throne and replace him with Charles's eldest illegitimate son, James, Duke of Monmouth. The Commons passed the bill, but the king dissolved Parliament before it could proceed to the Lords. In October 1680, the Commons passed a similar bill, but, after pressure from the king, it was defeated in the Lords.

Charles entered into secret negotiations with Louis XIV for new subsidies, with the result that when he summoned a new parliament to Oxford in 1681 he was financially independent. Yet another Exclusion Bill was passed, but the king again dissolved Parliament.

A failed plot to assassinate Charles at Rye House in April 1683 and to replace him with Monmouth introduced a Royalist backlash that allowed the king to dispense with Parliament for the rest of his reign, in contravention of the Triennial Act. By the time of his death, Charles had greatly increased the authority of the Crown.

Let Not Poor Nelly Starve

On 2 February 1685 Charles became ill, suffering an apoplectic fit while being shaved. His health rapidly deteriorated, although he patiently bore the bleedings and blisterings inflicted upon him by his physicians with his customary self-deprecating good humour, apologising 'for being such an unconscionable time a-dying'.

On 5 February the king made a confession of faith to the Roman Catholic Church, making his confession and receiving absolution and then receiving the sacrament of extreme unction from the elderly priest, Father John Huddleston.

Charles II died on Friday 6 February, entreating his brother James to care for his children and his mistresses, Louise, Duchess of Portsmouth, and Nell Gwynn.

Above left: Titus Oates in the stocks. (Author's collection)

Above right: Wax funeral effigy of Charles II. (Copyright Dean and Chapter of Westminster)

5
JAMES II
1685–1688

FLIGHT

On a cold December night in 1688, James II left Whitehall Palace to flee the country. Accompanied by Sir Edward Hales, the king took a small skiff down the Thames, throwing the Great Seal into the river. He had inherited a secure throne and a prosperous realm, but within three short years he had alienated his people, his Parliament and even his children, and so a second Stuart monarch was deposed.

The broken, fearful man who abandoned his country was a far cry from the brave, handsome prince who had been his mother's favourite, preferred by many to his brother Charles, and who had for a time been a national hero. Yet perhaps the fatal signs of the characteristics which contributed to the king's self-destruction had always been there.

A GOODLY, LUSTY CHILD

James Stuart was born on 14 October 1633, the second surviving son of King Charles I and his French wife, Henrietta Maria. The newsletter announcing his birth informed the public that the royal couple were 'well and jolly' at the birth of their son, who was baptised a month later by William Laud, the new Archbishop of Canterbury.

The young prince shared his nursery with his brother Charles, who was three years his senior but to whom he bore little resemblance – both physically and in character – and his sister Mary, the Princess Royal, born in 1631. They were joined two years later by Elizabeth and then by Anne in 1637, who died aged three. Princess Catherine survived only a day, but a third son, named Henry, was born in 1640. A final sister, Henrietta Anne, known as Minette, was born in 1644 during the Civil War.

James, tall, fair and blue-eyed, enjoyed the happy and pampered life of a royal prince, displaying a character known for both its sweetness and gentleness, but also strong-willed and stubborn, and lacking in the humour and wit which so characterised his elder brother Charles.

The secure and privileged existence of the royal children was shattered by the events of the Civil War, which began when James was only eight years old, considerably affecting his education. Too young to play any part in the war, the young prince spent almost all the time at the Court and Royalist headquarters in Oxford, being created Duke of York on 22 January 1644.

But as the war progressed, it became clear that the king was losing. James, alone of the royal family, remained in Oxford and became a prisoner when the city surrendered to the Parliamentary forces in 1646. He affected a daring escape from St James's Palace twenty months later and made his way to his sister Mary in Holland, the wife of Prince William of Orange.

A Soldier of Fortune

The events James lived through were seared into his memory, profoundly affecting his later character and actions. He became convinced that any who opposed the royal will must be punished, with no recourse to compromise. In particular, he developed a bitter mistrust of Parliament, which had shattered his happy life and murdered God's anointed king, his father.

James had been appointed Lord High Admiral at the age of three and this honorary role was confirmed by his brother Charles after the execution of their father, but, to James's chagrin, he was not permitted to sail with the fleet. He was then commissioned as an officer in the French army under Marshall Turenne against the Fronde and later against their Spanish allies, where he distinguished himself by his courage.

When the French government came to terms with the Cromwellian Protectorate, James resigned his commission and served, along with his younger brother Henry, Duke of Gloucester, with the Spaniards under Louis, Prince of Condé, fighting against the French.

After the French and Spanish made peace in 1659, James considered taking a Spanish offer to be an admiral in their navy. However, after the death of Cromwell and the disintegration of the Protectorate, the royalist fortunes dramatically changed and James returned to England with his brother Charles in May 1660.

An Unfortunate Marriage

On his return to England, James was embroiled in a scandal by announcing his engagement to Anne Hyde, who was the daughter of Charles's chief minister, Edward Hyde, and lady-in-waiting to his sister Mary. The marriage of a royal prince to a commoner was regarded with horror by all, including Hyde, now Earl of Clarendon, and the duke's mother, Henrietta Maria. Several courtiers were persuaded to come forward and claim that they too had been Anne's lovers and James hoped that he might evade marriage. However, Charles II ordered him to honour his contract of marriage and the couple married on 3 September 1660.

Their first child, Charles, was born less than two months later, but died in infancy, as did five further sons and daughters. Only two daughters survived: Mary, born in 1662, and Anne, born in 1665. James was a fond father, occasioning Samuel Pepys to note that the duke played with his children 'like an ordinary private father of a child'.

Anne was devoted to James and influenced many of his decisions. Even so, like his brother the king, the duke kept a variety of mistresses, including Arabella Churchill and Catherine Sedley, by whom he had a daughter; unlike Charles II, however, James experienced guilt over his infidelities. Some of these women were so plain that Charles remarked that they must have been recommended to James as a penance by his priests.

A COURAGEOUS PRINCE

After the Restoration, James was confirmed as Lord High Admiral, an office that carried with it the subsidiary appointments of Governor of Portsmouth and Lord Warden of the Cinque Ports. He commanded the Royal Navy during the Second and Third Anglo-Dutch Wars, becoming a hero at the Battle of Lowestoft in June 1665.

A foldable and adjustable birthing chair, made of walnut wood. European. Late seventeenth century. (Courtesy of Wellcome Library, London)

In September 1666, the king put James in charge of firefighting operations during the Great Fire of London and his courage won him praise; one witness wrote that 'The Duke of York hath won the hearts of the people with his continual and indefatigable pains day and night in helping to quench the Fire'.

CONVERSION TO ROMAN CATHOLICISM

Around 1668, James, like his wife Anne, secretly converted to Roman Catholicism. Growing fears of Catholic influence at court led to the introduction of a Test Act in 1673, whereby all civil and military officials were required to take an oath denying the doctrine of Transubstantiation and to receive the Eucharist under the auspices of the Church of England. James refused, and resigned his post as Lord High Admiral, making public his conversion to Catholicism.

Two years after the death of his first wife in 1671, James married the fifteen-year-old Catholic Italian princess, Mary of Modena, by proxy in a Catholic ceremony. The marriage increased the duke's unpopularity, and many regarded the new Duchess of York as an agent of the Pope.

EXCLUSION CRISIS

In 1677, James reluctantly consented to the marriage of his eldest daughter Mary to his nephew, the Protestant William of Orange. William was born on 14 November 1650, which was the nineteenth birthday of his mother Mary Stuart and eight days after the death of his father from smallpox. The young William was groomed to lead the powerful House of Orange and to become a *Stadtholder*, or head of state, of the Dutch Republic.

The failure of Charles II and his wife Catherine of Braganza to produce an heir to the throne, leaving James as his successor, exacerbated anti-Catholic agitation;

Late seventeenth-century Dutch clay pipe. (P. J. Womack. Author's collection)

this culminated in the so-called Popish Plot, in which Titus Oates claimed that there was a Jesuit conspiracy to kill the king and to put the Duke of York on the throne. The fabricated plot caused a wave of hysteria to sweep across the nation.

The Earl of Shaftesbury and other leading Whigs attempted to introduce an Exclusion Bill to exclude James from succession to the throne, but Charles dissolved Parliament and then sent James firstly to Brussels and then to Edinburgh. He returned to England when the king was taken seriously ill in 1682 and brought an action for libel against Oates.

THE RYE HOUSE PLOT

In 1683 a conspiracy to assassinate Charles and James and bring about a revolution was uncovered. Several notable Whigs and the king's eldest illegitimate son, James Scott, Duke of Monmouth, were implicated. Monmouth, along with several others, was obliged to flee into Continental exile. Taking advantage of sympathy for James, Charles invited him back onto the Privy Council and the Committee for Foreign affairs.

ACCESSION TO THE THRONE

James was fifty-two when he succeeded to the throne as James II of England and James VII of Scotland, in February 1685. His accession was accepted peacefully amid widespread reports of public rejoicing, and he was crowned at Westminster Abbey on 23 April 1685. James's first Parliament in May 1685, known as the 'Loyal Parliament', was initially favourable to him and voted him a generous revenue. In return, the new king promised to rule by the established laws and to maintain the independence of the Church of England.

THE MONMOUTH REBELLION

Two months after his coronation, James faced a rebellion in southern England led by his nephew, the Duke of Monmouth, and another rebellion led by Archibald Campbell, the Earl of Argyll, who sailed from Holland and invaded Scotland. Both leaders had wrongly assumed that their countries would support the overthrow of a Catholic king and Argyle's rebellion was

SEVENTEENTH-CENTURY RECIPES

The popularity of toast is nothing new. Here are several recipes from *The Accomplisht Cook*, written by Robert May around 1685:

Toasts of Divers Sorts
First, in Butter or Oyl.
    Take a cast of fine rouls or round manchet, chip them, and cut them into toasts, fry them in clarified butter, frying oyl, or sallet oyl, but before you fry them dip them in fair water, and being fried, serve them in a clean dish piled one upon another, and sugar between.
    Other ways.
Toste them before the fire, and run them over with butter, sugar, or oyl.
    Cinamon Toast.
Cut fine thin toasts, then toast them on a gridiron, and lay them in ranks in a dish, put to them fine beaten cinamon mixed with sugar and some claret, warm them over the fire, and serve them hot.
    French Toast.
Cut French bread, and toast it in pretty thick toasts on a clean gridiron, and serve them steeped in claret, sack, or any wine, with sugar and juyce of orange.

put down with relative ease. Monmouth claimed to represent the Protestant cause, but his forces were defeated at Sedgemoor on 6 July.

Monmouth's capture and execution was followed by the brutal suppression of his followers by Lord Chief Justice George Jeffreys, known as the Hanging Judge, and became known as the 'Bloody Assizes'.

A PAPIST KING

James determined to build up a military force of such strength as would make further revolts impossible, and the royal army grew to almost 30,000. Half these were encamped on Hounslow Heath, west of London, dominating the capital. In garrison towns such as Hull, the brutality of martial law was

Mezzotint of James Scott, Duke of
Monmouth, by Jan van der Vaart, after
Edward Cooper. (Courtesy of Rijksmuseum,
Amsterdam)

imposed on the civilian population, while the army was protected from being
brought to account for offences against the civilians. This was accompanied
by a campaign against the carrying of arms by private individuals.

Even more alarming to Parliament were James's attempts to win converts
among the ranks of soldiers and his appointment of Roman Catholics as officers,
in defiance of the Test Act. Equally worrying was the enlistment of Catholic
troops in Ireland, who were brought over to England.

Fears of arbitrary government were heightened further by the revocation of the
Edict of Nantes in 1685 by Louis XIV, which had allowed freedom of worship
to France's one million Protestant Huguenots. Over 50,000 fled to England with
horrific stories of their sufferings. Parliament petitioned James to reduce his army
and dismiss the Catholic officers, but the king's response was to order Parliament
prorogued in November 1685 and dissolved in July 1687.

Faced with the refusal of Parliament to provide religious freedom and legal
equality for Catholics, James proceeded to establish their rights by royal
prerogative. He appointed an ecclesiastical commission to prevent Anglican
clergy from attacking the Roman Catholic religion from their pulpits. When the
Bishop of London disobeyed this order, he was suspended from his office.

This was followed by a test case which decided that it was legal for the king to dispense with the law in individual cases and dismiss judges who disagreed. This resulted in the appointment of Catholics to the Privy Council, to the magistracy, for positions in Oxford colleges, and as military and naval officers.

In Ireland, the king replaced the Protestant Earl of Clarendon with the English Catholic Richard Talbot, Earl of Tyrconnell, as Lord Lieutenant, who filled the ranks of James's army in Ireland with Catholics. Catholic judges were also appointed and the policies accelerated in January 1667 when Tyrconnell became Lord Deputy. Writs were used to give Catholics a two-third majority in most corporations, ensuring that a future Irish Parliament would be overwhelmingly Catholic, and revenues of the Church of Ireland were redirected to fund Catholics.

Similar policies were used in Scotland, where Catholics were placed within the army. James dissolved the Scottish Parliament for failing to agree to religious toleration and in February 1687 a proclamation was issued that granted freedom of worship to Catholics and Quakers but excluded Presbyterians.

THE BISHOPS IN THE TOWER

The king's pro-French alliance created the strong impression of his intention to reign as an absolute Catholic monarch like Louis XIV. In 1687 James issued the Declaration of Indulgence, in which he used his dispensing power to negate the effect of laws punishing Catholics and Protestant Dissenters. At the same time, he provided partial toleration in Scotland, using his dispensing power to grant relief to Catholics and partial relief to Presbyterians. Borough charters were remodelled and Catholics were set up as magistrates. An ecclesiastical commission was set up to act as a court for Church affairs, with power to make and unmake appointments and property settlements. Although this was technically illegal after the abolition of the Court of High Commission in 1641, James used it in 1687 to expel the fellows of Magdalen College, Oxford, and replace them with Catholics; this was an act which was viewed as an attack upon the Church, the Protestant religion and the security of law and property.

The summer of 1688 was the turning point in the king's reign. In June James renewed the Declaration of Indulgence, ordering that this be read from the pulpit in every parish. When William Sancroft, Archbishop of Canterbury, and six other bishops refused, they were charged with sedition, confined in the Tower and put on trial. Their subsequent acquittal was cause for public celebration and prompted the emergence of an alliance of Anglicans and Dissenters against the king.

THE WARMING-PAN PRINCE

Two days later, James's wife, Mary of Modena, gave birth to a son named James Francis Edward. Up until then, the king's opponents had known that James's Protestant daughter would inherit the throne. The birth of a son now ensured a Catholic succession and meant that Mary, the wife of William of Orange, was no longer the heir to the throne. The king's two daughters claimed that the child was an imposter who had been smuggled into the queen's bedchamber.

James's announcement that he wished the Pope to be his son's godfather was a further indication of how divorced he was from the fears of his people.

A WITCH TRIAL

Fear of witchcraft and witch trials continued long after the reign of James's grandfather, as this letter shows:

> A poor old woman had the hard fate to be condemned as a witch. Some, that were more apt to believe those things than me, thought the evidence strong against her, the boy that said he was bewitched falling into fits before the bench when he see her. But in all this it was observed that the boy had no distortion, no foaming at the mouth, nor did his fits leave him gradually, but all of a sudden; so that the judge thought fit to reprieve her.
>
> However, it is just to relate this odd story. One of my soldiers, being upon the guard at eleven o'clock at Clifford Tower Gate the night the witch was arraigned, hearing a great noise at the Castle, came to the porch, and being there see a scroll of paper creep from under the door, which, as he imagined by moonshine, turned first into the shape of a monkey, then a turkey cock, which moved to and fro by him. Where upon he went to the gaol and called the under-gaoler, who came and see the scroll dance up and down and creep under the door, where there was scarce the room of a thickness of half a crown. This I had from the mouth both of the soldier and the gaoler.
>
> Sir John Reresby at the York Assizes in 1687.

THE INVASION OF WILLIAM OF ORANGE

On the day that the seven bishops were acquitted, seven leading Protestants, representing both Whig and Tory opinion and including Bishop Compton, Bishop of London, met and wrote a letter to William of Orange, inviting him to intervene in English affairs. This was not an invitation to take the throne, but was an indication of how many factions James had alienated.

The invitation came as no surprise to William, who was consumed with the desire to combat Catholic France; the Dutch had already been making preparations for a military invasion of England. William had been organising an English fifth column for over a year, and was kept informed of disaffection in the king's military, gaining specific pledges of support from commanders in both the army and the navy. An important consideration was that the invasion offered the only way of securing English assistance for a Dutch republic threatened with extinction by James's ally, Louis XIV, and the rulers of the republic agreed to finance and equip an army for William.

James was unaware of his son-in-law's intentions and did not seriously entertain the notion that his daughter Mary would agree to an unprovoked attack. In August 1688, the king ordered the issue of writs for a general election. However, upon realising that Dutch military preparations were directed at him and not at Louis XIV, James withdrew the writs and endeavoured to generate support by announcing that no Catholics would be allowed to sit in the upcoming Parliament, abolishing the new Court of High Commission, dismissing many Catholics from office and restating the former fellows of Magdalen College. To the Dutch, he offered English neutrality. It was too late.

With Louis XIV occupied in an invasion of the Palatinate, William of Orange took advantage of a strong, easterly 'Protestant wind', which enabled him to sail along the Channel but kept James's fleet in port. When he arrived on 5 November 1688, the day on which the country celebrated its deliverance from the Gunpowder Plot, many Protestant officers, including two of James's leading commanders, his nephew, the Duke of Grafton, and John Churchill, defected to him.

Worse was to follow, for the king's youngest daughter Anne slipped out of Whitehall and fled to the Midlands; her husband George, Prince of Denmark, had already absconded from James's army. Betrayed by his children, his bishops, his lords and his leading officers, the king exclaimed, 'God help me! My own children have forsaken me.'

The Man of War Brielle *on the River Maas off Rotterdam* by Ludolf Bakhuysen, 1689. This ship carried William of Orange to England. The Latin inscription on the red flag translates as 'for faith and freedom.' (Courtesy of Rijksmuseum, Amsterdam)

Suffering from severe nosebleeds, James lost his nerve and declined to attack the invading army, despite his army's numerical superiority. The king was advised by his remaining peers to call Parliament and offer a pardon to William and his supporters, and James sent Halifax, Nottingham and Godolphin to negotiate. William received the king's overtures coolly and James, remembering the fate of his father, made plans to flee. He sent the queen and the Prince of Wales to safety in France, where he planned to join them. James was captured in Kent, but allowed to escape to France, where he was received by his cousin and ally, Louis XIV, who offered him a palace at Saint-Germain-en-Laye and a pension.

THE KING OVER THE WATER

James made an attempt to regain his throne two years later by invading Ireland, but was decisively defeated by William at the Battle of the Boyne on 1 July 1690.

The king spent the rest of his life in exile, devoting himself to prayer, fasting and penances, and died on 16 September 1701. Perhaps this comment from the

French court best sums him up, that 'our good King James is a brave and honest man, but the silliest I have ever seen in my life; a child of seven would not make such crass mistakes as he does'.

Right: A lost cause: The Flight of James II after the Battle of the Boyne, 1690 by Andrew C. Gow. (Author's collection)

Below: The Château de Saint-Germain-en-Laye. James II lived in the château for thirteen years, and his daughter Louise-Marie Stuart was born in exile here in 1692. (Author's collection)

6

WILLIAM III AND MARY II 1689–1702 & 1689–1694

THE GLORIOUS REVOLUTION

The joint accession to the throne of William of Orange and Princess Mary, daughter of James II, on 13 February 1689, marked the first time in English history that a royal succession had been settled by Parliament, not by hereditary right, by conquest or possession of the crown. It brought into being a constitutional monarchy which was subject to Parliament.

On 23 December 1688, the day on which James II escaped to France, the peers and bishops of the House of Lords requested that William of Orange assume the duties of government. On 28 January 1689, the Commons declared that James II had abdicated by leaving the kingdom and that the throne was therefore vacant. The Protestant Whigs in the Commons were largely in favour of the throne passing to William and Mary; however, in the Lords, the Tory supporters of absolute monarchy were determined to safeguard the principle of hereditary succession and believed that Mary should rule alone.

Although his wife ranked higher in the line of succession to the throne, William was determined to reign as king in his own right, with the full power and sovereignty of a monarch, rather than as a mere consort, stating that he would not be tied by apron strings, nor would he agree to be a regent or to remaining king only in his wife's lifetime. The Crown was not offered to James's eldest son, James Francis Edward, but to William and Mary as joint sovereigns, with the proviso that 'the sole and full exercise of the regal power be only in and executed by the said Prince of Orange in the names of the said Prince and Princess during their joint lives'.

THE DECLARATION OF RIGHTS

Parliament's immediate concern after the accession was to draw up the basis for a future settlement and William and Mary were asked to agree to a list of demands set out by Parliament known as a Declaration of Rights. There were several

Above left: *William III and Mary II* by Peter Hoadly. (Courtesy of Rijksmuseum, Amsterdam)

Above right: *Mary II as child,* attributed to Richard Gibson, 1665–75. (Courtesy of Rijksmuseum, Amsterdam)

conditions: the sovereign must never again keep a standing army in peacetime without Parliament's consent and Parliament had the authority in declaring war, raising taxes and passing laws. Free elections to Parliament would be held every three years and MPs were guaranteed free speech. In addition, all Protestants were allowed to carry arms for self-defence. Most significantly, the sovereign must neither be, nor marry, a Catholic. These conditions were later enacted in the Bill of Rights in December 1689 and others in later Acts such as the Toleration Act and the Triennial Act of 1694. Parliament was to grant the Crown a fairly small sum for ordinary revenue, and was to grant it for only one year at a time.

Unlike the settlement of 1660, this financial settlement was deliberately made inadequate in order to ensure dependence of the sovereign upon Parliament. The bill also specified the future succession; firstly through Mary, then through her sister Anne and her heirs and then through any heirs of William by a subsequent marriage.

On 11 April 1689, King William III and Queen Mary II were crowned at Westminster Abbey by the Bishop of London, Henry Compton; William Sancroft,

Archbishop of Canterbury, refused to recognise James's removal, despite his being one of the seven bishops who had been arrested by James for refusing to accept the Declaration of Indulgence. The new monarchs were compelled to swear oaths that required them to uphold the Protestant reformed religion established by law and to govern in accordance with the Statutes of Parliament.

Although most people in England accepted William and Mary as sovereigns, a significant minority refused to accept the validity of their claim to the throne, holding that the Divine Right of kings was authority directly given by God, not delegated to the monarch by Parliament.

Over the next fifty-seven years, Jacobites – or supporters of James II, taken from the Latin form of the name, Jacobus – pressed for the restoration of the king and his heirs. Many of the Anglican clergy felt legally bound by their previous oaths of allegiance to King James, and over 400 clergy and several bishops of the Church of England and Scottish Episcopal Church, as well as numerous laymen, refused to take oaths of allegiance to William.

SCOTLAND

In Scotland, the Parliament offered the throne to William and Mary, accompanying this by a Claim of Right, which declared that the Crown should relinquish control of the Church of Scotland through bishops and should recognise it as fully Presbyterian. William agreed, and his government was soon in full control of the Lowlands. However, in the Highlands, the old loyalties to Catholicism and the House of Stuart were strong and here a movement developed, headed by John Graham of Claverhouse, Viscount Dundee, who was known as 'Bonnie Dundee'.

The movement gained strength, and when government forces marched north, Dundee led a force of highlanders in a famous victory over a royalist army commanded by General Hugh Mackay in the valley of Killiecrankie on 27 July 1689. Dundee was killed by a musket shot, and without his driving force the Jacobite cause foundered; the royalist forces inflicted a decisive defeat on the Jacobites at Dunkeld on 21 August.

THE MASSACRE AT GLENCOE

By the end of 1689, William was generally acknowledged throughout Scotland, but parts of the Highlands were not under control. The government ordered a number of chiefs to take an oath of allegiance by 31 December 1691, but Alastair

HOW TO GET AHEAD AT COURT

The headdress of a fashionable lady from this period evolved from a white lace or silk cap, with a fan of wired, fluted lace standing up in front, requiring a wire frame known as a commode to support it.

The curled hair was piled up in high masses over the forehead over the frame. The 'fontage' or 'tower' consisted of alternate layers of lace and ribbon raised one above another about half a yard high, named after Mademoiselle Fontages, one of Louis XIV's mistresses, who introduced it to France in 1679.

The fontages could also be arranged to indicate political preferences and had lace and ribbons added. Long lappets fell down the back, and sapphire or diamond bodkins and ribbon bows, and probably lice, completed the ensemble.

MacIain, the chief of the MacDonald clan, was late in responding. William's chief Scottish adviser, the Master of Stair, took MacIain's lateness as an opportunity to teach the troublesome MacDonald clan a lesson. Supported by the Campbell clan, he informed William that MacIain had failed to appear by the appointed time and received permission to inflict punishment, leading to the brutal massacre at Glencoe on 13 February 1692. Public outrage, and the fact that William did not try to punish those responsible, undermined his popularity.

THE BATTLE OF THE BOYNE

In Ireland, James II's Catholic deputy, the Earl of Tyrconnell, had retained control of the country on his behalf. The Protestants of Ulster supported William, but were forced to take refuge in Enniskillen and Londonderry. Three months later, James landed in Ireland with an army of 20,000 French soldiers, boosted by large numbers of Irish Catholics, to reassert his title to the throne. He called a Parliament on 4 May 1689, in which the majority were Catholics, which passed an Act of Attainder against around 2,000 leading Protestants.

At first, James swept Protestant opposition aside, but found the gates closed against him at Londonderry and embarked on a lengthy siege. Thousands of lives were lost as the city grimly stuck to their slogan of 'no surrender', until English troops broke the boom on the River Foyle and relieved the siege. Shortly afterwards, the garrison at Enniskillen also won a notable victory.

William landed at Carrick Fergus on 24 June 1690 and on 1 July, at the head of a vast army of 36,000 soldiers, he inflicted a decisive defeat on James's forces at the Battle of the Boyne.

James fled again to France and William returned to England, appointing John Churchill, Duke of Marlborough, to command the royalist forces in Ireland.

The war continued for another fifteen months until the last Irish forces were defeated at Limerick, and the Peace of Limerick was signed on 3 October 1691. William's Parliaments in England and Ireland imposed severe restrictions on Catholics, including not being able to vote at elections, sit in Parliament or town corporations or serve as jurymen, soldiers or schoolmasters.

WAR WITH FRANCE

William's overriding concern was the defence of Holland against France. With Louis XIV supporting his cousin James II, William allied England with the League of Augsburg, which afterwards became known as the Grand Alliance. In 1690, the French defeated an Anglo-Dutch fleet off Beachy Head. However, two years later, the Allies won a decisive victory at La Hogue in 1692 under Admiral Russell and for the rest of the war no French battle fleet put to sea, while the Allies enjoyed the advantages of naval superiority,

QUEEN MARY

William was never really a popular king; he was distrusted as a foreigner and his cold and aloof manner and unattractive appearance did not endear him with his subjects, unlike his wife. Mary was admired for her beauty and statuesque figure and, at 1.8 m, she was a full twelve centimetres taller than her husband.

The queen was a devout Protestant and was believed to epitomise the perfect model of a dutiful wife, being content to leave affairs of state and government to William. Despite Mary's view that women should not meddle in government, her husband's frequent absences from the realm meant that she ruled as regnant queen for a total of thirty-two months when William was abroad on campaign in Ireland and Flanders. Her competency and sound judgment, particularly after the military defeat at Beachy Head in 1690, led some news sheets to claim that she was a new Elizabeth.

Above left: Two flower holders, A. De Griekschc, Adrianus Kocx, *c.* 1690–1700. Flower holders like these examples are thought to have belonged to Mary II. (Courtesy of Rijksmuseum, Amsterdam)

Above right: Bust of Mary Stuart, A. De Grieksche, Samuel van Eenhoorn, *c.* 1680–1690, made from tin-glazed earthenware. Mary was particularly fond of this material and De Grieksche was her favourite supplier. (Courtesy of Rijksmuseum, Amsterdam)

DEATH OF MARY 1694

Mary II died of smallpox on 28 December 1694 aged thirty-two, leaving her grief-stricken husband to rule alone. Through the years, the royal couple had developed a genuine affection for each other and the king risked infection to be with her on her deathbed. For a month, William's sorrow so prostrated him that there were fears for his health, and he ended his long-standing affair with Elizabeth Villiers, Mary's lady-in-waiting.

The queen's funeral procession was the largest and most expensive ever held for an English monarch. William's concern was not only for the personal loss of his wife; he believed that her untimely death was God's judgment on his sins, and in this belief he was not alone. The queen had been popular and admired by the people in a way he never had and, most importantly, her death removed the argument that William enjoyed a 'hereditary right by proxy' to the English throne.

Mary's demise, the increasingly unpopular war in Europe and hostility from Parliament and Church meant that William's reign was at crisis point.

MUSIC FIT FOR A QUEEN

Henry Purcell (1659–1695) is considered to be England's greatest composer of the Baroque era. He was born in London, the son of Thomas Purcell, one of the king's musicians, and attended Westminster School. In 1674, he was appointed tuner of Westminster Abbey. He was appointed copyist in 1676 and succeeded Matthew Locke as 'composer to the King's violins' the following year.

Aged only twenty, Purcell was awarded the prestigious post of Organist of Westminster Abbey in 1679, and in the following year he published his Fantasias for strings and began to compose the long series of 'welcome odes' and other official choral pieces. Purcell wrote incidental music for the theatre for Dryden, who described him as 'an Englishman, equal with the best abroad'. In 1682, Purcell became one of the three organists of the Chapel Royal and his sonatas in three parts were published the next year.

The anthem 'My Heart is Inditing' was written for the coronation of King James II on 23 April 1685 and Purcell was again involved in a royal occasion when he played at the coronation of William III and Mary II on 11 April 1689.

As a favourite composer of the king, Purcell was called upon to compose odes for the birthdays of Queen Mary, concluding with 'Come, Ye Sons of Art, Away' in 1694. His first opera, *Dido and Aeneas*, based on Book IV of Virgil's *Aeneid*, was composed in 1689.

In the last few years of his life, Purcell was increasingly prolific, composing some of his greatest church music. In 1695, he performed his last duty for the queen when he composed the anthem 'Thou Knowest, Lord, the Secrets of our Hearts' for her funeral.

Purcell died at the age of thirty-six, probably from tuberculosis, and was buried next to the organ in Westminster Abbey. His epitaph reads, 'Here lyes Henry Purcell Esq., who left this life and is gone to that blessed place where only his harmony can be exceeded.'

A DUTCH KING ON AN ENGLISH THRONE

The reign of William III marked steps towards party government. Because the Tories were more supportive of his rights, the king at first drew most of his ministers from them. But, as the war with France dragged on, William turned to the Whigs, who were more supportive of its continuation.

William was far from being a figurehead; he chose his own ministers and made treaties without divulging all the details in advance, five times refusing to consent to bills which had been passed by both Houses of Parliament. However, he was forced to agree to other measures, such as a Triennial Act, which ensured a new Parliament was called every three years.

PEACE

In 1697, Louis XIV agreed peace terms favourable to the Grand Alliance. This was partly because of the question of who would succeed to the throne of the childless Spanish king, Charles II. Peace was made in 1697 with the Treaty of Ryswick, in which Louis agreed to restore all conquests except Strasbourg, to recognise William as King of England and to give no support to his enemies, including James II. In addition, the Dutch were to be allowed to garrison a number of towns in the Spanish Netherlands to form a barrier against any further French aggression.

The end of the war was celebrated in England by a spectacular firework display in St James's Square, in which several spectators were killed.

The long years of fighting cost William's government around £40 million. Parliament had been prepared to vote the necessary money because of its agreement that Louis XIV must be resisted. Such large amounts would have been impossible to raise by ordinary taxation and new customs duties and a new land tax had helped to increase revenue, but the government still needed to borrow on a larger scale than ever before. This led to the formation of the Bank of England in 1694.

THE ACT OF SETTLEMENT 1701

After the Treaty of Ryswick, Parliament insisted that William's army should be cut, his Dutch guard dismissed and his grants of land to his Dutch friends cancelled. In addition, a measure known as the Act of Settlement limited the future rights of foreigners and foreign-born monarchs in England.

The main purpose of the Act was to provide for the succession. Mary had died childless, suffering miscarriages in 1678 and 1679; although her sister Anne was recognised as heir to the throne, she was middle-aged and in poor health and her last surviving son, William, Duke of Gloucester, had just died.

The Act laid down that, after Anne's death, the Crown should pass to the Electress Sophia of Hanover and her heirs; she was the daughter of James I's daughter, Elizabeth, and Frederick V, the Elector Palatine. James II's descendants were barred from the throne.

The Act also stated that receipt of the Anglican Eucharist was compulsory for all monarchs, and that future sovereigns would not be permitted to launch a war 'for the defence of dominions or territories which do not belong to the Crown of England without the consent of Parliament' and would not be permitted to depart from England without Parliamentary consent; this was a measure which reflected concern at William's frequent absences from the realm.

JACOBITE PLOTS

In 1697, a failed Jacobite assassination plot rallied public opinion in William's favour. Parliament passed the Act of Association, in which all holders of public office were required to swear that William was the right and lawful king and it was declared high treason to travel from France to England without official authority.

Following the death of James II on 6 September 1701, Louis XIV recognised James's son, James Francis Edward, known as the 'Pretender', as the rightful king of England, in direct contravention of the treaty. In the previous April, the Commons had voted to support the Dutch against the French and, two months later, to ally with Austria and the United Provinces. English opinion was in favour of another war with France and, on 7 September at The Hague, William agreed to ally England with the Netherlands and the Holy Roman Empire. The subsequent conflict, known as the War of the Spanish Succession, continued until 1713.

DEATH OF WILLIAM 1702

On 21 February 1702, while riding in Hyde Park, William was thrown from his horse after it tripped over a molehill and he broke his collarbone. The king appeared to make a good recovery, but collapsed while walking in the gallery at Kensington House on 5 March. William developed pulmonary fever and died on 8 March 1702.

After his death, Jacobites toasted the mole, 'the little gentleman in his black velvet jacket', who had contributed to the demise of their enemy.

William III by Godfried
Schalken, *c.* 1692–97. (Courtesy
of Rijksmuseum, Amsterdam)

7

ANNE
1702–1714

THE LAST STUART

On St George's Day, 23 April 1702, Princess Anne, the last monarch from the Royal House of Stuart, was crowned queen in Westminster Abbey. Troubled by gout and rheumatism, thirty-seven-year-old Anne had to be carried to her coronation in a sedan chair by the Yeomen of the Guard. Although the sight of the plain, corpulent woman, with her pitted skin and bulging, watery eyes was unlikely to arouse admiration, the queen became beloved of her people.

Anne presided over a great period in the history of her country, during which English forces won resounding victories over the French and re-established England as a significant European power with growing imperial possessions. Under Anne, England became a major military and naval power, the kingdoms of England and Scotland were formally joined in the kingdom of Great Britain and in decorative arts the country reached a new height of elegance with the development of the Queen Anne style.

EARLY YEARS

Anne was born on 6 February 1665 at St James's Palace, the fourth child and second daughter of James, Duke of York, and his first wife, Anne Hyde, the daughter of Lord Chancellor Edward Hyde, 1st Earl of Clarendon. The Duke and Duchess of York had eight children, but Anne and Mary were the only ones to survive into adulthood.

As a child, Anne suffered from an eye condition known as defluxion, which caused excessive watering. She was sent to France for medical treatment, where she lived with her grandmother, the dowager queen, Henrietta Maria, at the Château de Colombes near Paris. Following her grandmother's death in 1669, Anne lived with Henrietta Anne, Duchess of Orleans, who was her father's youngest sister and who was known as Minette. When her aunt suddenly died in 1670, Anne returned to England. Her mother, Anne Hyde, died the following year.

MRS MORLEY

Anne and her elder sister Mary were brought up in their own establishment at Richmond, London. On the instructions of their uncle, King Charles II, they were raised as Protestants and placed in the care of Colonel Edward and Lady Frances Villiers. Anne's relations with Mary were frequently poor; the two were dissimilar in character, with Anne naturally taciturn and gloomy. However, she enjoyed intense friendships with other woman, notably with Sarah Jennings, whom she met around 1671 and who became her intimate friend and one of her most influential advisors. Anne conceived of the idea of the two women using pseudonyms in their frequent letters to one another and for over twenty years they corresponded as 'Mrs Morley' and 'Mrs Freeman'. Sarah married John Churchill, the future Duke of Marlborough around 1678, whose sister Arabella was the Duke of York's mistress.

Below left: Queen Anne by Charles Boit. (Courtesy of Rijksmuseum, Amsterdam)

Below right: Lithograph of Queen Anne by Rosalind Thornycroft, 1933. (Author's collection)

A Happy Marriage

On 4 November 1677 Mary married their Dutch cousin, William of Orange, at St James's Palace. Ill with smallpox, Anne could not attend the wedding and by the time she had recovered Mary had already left for her new life. The death of her governess, Lady Frances Villiers, from smallpox, increased Anne's emotional dependency on Sarah.

King Charles II now began a search for a suitable husband for Anne. Several Protestant princes were considered, including Prince George of Hanover, who later succeeded Anne as George I. The prince was not impressed with Anne and left the country without making an offer of marriage, a slight Anne did not forget. However, a match was arranged with the thirty-year-old Prince George of Denmark, the younger brother of King Christian V, and the seventeen-year-old Anne was given away in marriage by the king on 28 July 1683. The couple was well-suited and they remained faithful and devoted to one another throughout their married life.

Good-looking, genial and rather dull, the prince had a reputation as a brave soldier and had once saved his elder brother's life, but he was treated with contempt by his brother-in-law William and by Charles II, who commented, 'I have tried him drunk and I have tried him sober, but there is nothing in him.' Of Anne's seventeen pregnancies, twelve resulted in miscarriages, one in a stillbirth and she bore four children who did not survive infancy. Her son William, Duke of Gloucester, upon whom she doted, died at the age of eleven.

A Family Divided

Although Anne initially got on well with her stepmother, Mary of Modena, whom her father had married in 1673, their relationship deteriorated, particularly as the devoutly Protestant Anne disliked her stepmother's proselytising Catholicism. Mary and Anne were second and third in the line of succession after their father and were greatly dismayed by the birth of their father's son in the summer of 1688, encouraging the belief that he was an imposter and had been slipped into the queen's bed in a warming pan.

Anne welcomed the Dutch invasion of William of Orange and deserted her father, King James II, by slipping out of Whitehall Palace by night with Sarah Churchill and joining with William's supporters, even though she personally detested him. Anne's dislike of William was intensified by William's distrust of Marlborough and both she and Sarah referred to him as 'Mr Caliban'. Queen Mary's death in

1694 made it necessary for William to be on good terms with Anne, as she was his successor, and Marlborough was again admitted to his favour.

GOOD QUEEN ANNE

National mourning after the death of William III was brief and most of Anne's new subjects were relieved at having an English sovereign once more. Unlike William, Anne enjoyed the affection and respect of the nation. The new queen inherited a war with France and a monarchy financially dependent on Parliament, which was divided between Whigs, who supported limited monarchy and were aligned with Protestant Dissenters, and Tories, who favoured a strong monarchy and were supportive of the Anglican Church and the landed interests of the country gentry. They were also divided over support or opposition to wars and foreign policy, economic and religious concerns and the issue of the succession.

For the Tories, Anne was the rightful heir to the throne and a devout member of the Church of England and was, as she stressed in her first speech to Parliament, wholly English.

Anne lacked William's talent and experience of government, but, although her abilities were limited, she was extremely conscientious and, having failed to produce a child which survived to adulthood, she became a mother to her people. In 1704, the queen established 'Queen Anne's Bounty', which allowed the Church to retain fees formerly paid to the government and which was for the benefit of the poorer clergy; this act was remembered by churchmen long after her death.

Anne resumed elaborate Stuart ceremonies and revived the practice of touching for the king's evil in the Banqueting House, the site of the execution of Charles I, who was elevated into a cult figure during her reign. She enjoyed the ritual and display of the state opening of Parliament and thanksgiving services, deliberately drawing the parallel with herself and Elizabeth I, adopting Gloriana's motto, *semper eadem* (ever the same), as her own and dressing in imitation of her. As her generals recaptured the military glory associated with Elizabeth, the comparison grew stronger. However, Anne lacked Elizabeth's charisma and was greatly overweight; her pleasures were limited to gambling and dining. Like Elizabeth, she had to contend with men who attempted to dominate her, but she lacked the former's political intelligence.

Anne has often been portrayed as a weak ruler, but it seems unlikely that she was a mere pawn in a male political world and, although some made the mistake of underestimating her, she proved a more able and astute ruler than many had imagined.

THE GREAT STORM OF 1703

The week-long hurricane that struck the south of England and the English Channel on 26 November 1703 remains the worst in British history. It raged for a week, demolishing buildings, uprooting trees and sinking ships, and it was estimated that one-fifth of sailors in the Royal Navy were drowned.

In London over 2,000 chimney stacks were blown down, the lead roofing was blown off Westminster Abbey and Queen Anne took shelter in a cellar at St James's Palace to avoid collapsing chimneys.

Over 8,000 people lost their lives, along with thousands of sheep and cattle, while coastal towns were laid waste and the Eddystone Lighthouse off Plymouth was swept away, killing six occupants. At Wells, the fury of the storm blew in part of the great west window in Wells Cathedral and the chimneys of Wells Palace fell in, killing Bishop Richard Kidder and his wife in their bed.

Over 4,000 oak trees were uprooted in the New Forest alone and the diarist John Evelyn lost more than 2,000 on his estate in Surrey, describing the storm in his diary as 'not to be paralleled with anything happening in our age or in any history almost … every moment like Job's messengers brings the sad tidings of this universal judgment.'

Daniel Defoe, the author of *Robinson Crusoe*, narrowly avoided death in the street when part of a nearby house fell down. His book *The Storm*, which was published the following year, was the first detailed account of a hurricane in Britain.

It was generally believed that the storm was a visitation of the anger of God and Queen Anne's government announced that the calamity 'loudly calls for the deepest and most solemn humiliation of our people', proclaiming a national day of fasting and public prayer on 16 December.

Then, as now, climate change was a matter of grave concern. On the previous May, the vicar of Cheshunt in Hertfordshire had preached on the strange unseasonableness of the weather, attributing it to sin and exhorting his flock to repent.

The Great Storm was the first weather event to be a news story on a national scale. Special-issue broadsheets were produced, detailing damage to property and stories of people who had been killed.

The queen attended Privy Council meetings assiduously, even when in severe pain and when she had to be carried to meetings. Most importantly, Anne provided a focus for national unity and pride during the war with France.

POLITICS

Party politics became more significant throughout Anne's reign, with Whigs and Tories competing for power. Her first ministry was predominantly Tory, headed by the Lord Treasurer, Sydney, 1st Earl of Godolphin, and Anne's favourite, the Duke of Marlborough; they, along with the Speaker of the House of Commons, Robert Harley, 1st Earl of Oxford and Mortimer, were considered moderate Tories.

Anne supported the Occasional Conformity Bill of 1702, which was promoted by the Tories, who were alarmed by the large numbers of Dissenting meetings licensed under the Toleration Act of 1689 and regarded these as a threat to both the State and the Church. They resented the fact that Dissenters had found a loophole in the Test Act that prevented Dissenters from holding public office, as the existing law permitted nonconformists to take office if they took Anglican communion once a year. As most Dissenters were Whigs, the Tories and High Churchmen believed that toleration had gone too far. Two attempts were made in Parliament to outlaw occasional conformity, but each time these were defeated in the House of Lords, with the votes of Whig bishops preventing the bills from being passed. The queen's husband, Prince George, who as a Lutheran was an occasional conformist, was placed in the embarrassing position of being forced to vote for the Bill.

WAR WITH FRANCE

For most of Anne's reign, England was involved in the war of the Grand Alliance against France. In 1702 the continental conflict that had ended following the Treaty of Ryswick in 1697 was reignited, largely as a result of Louis XIV's support of James II's son, James Francis Edward Stuart, in his claim for the English throne. On 4 May 1702, England declared war against France, provoking Louis to comment wryly that 'it means I'm growing old when ladies declare war on me'.

The English army and navy won a series of battles, most famously at Blenheim in August 1704, a victory which was hailed by contemporaries as a new Agincourt. Marlborough was rewarded with a victory parade in London and the gift of the former royal manor of Woodstock, Oxfordshire, where Blenheim Palace was built. The war continued until 1713 and one of its enduring consequences was the British possession of Gibraltar in southern Spain.

'I HAVE THE SAME OPINION OF WHIG AND TORY THAT I EVER HAD'

The more extreme Tories became critical of Marlborough, because they favoured naval warfare rather than costly continental campaigns on land. Anne was upset by the criticism and raised Marlborough to a dukedom, requesting that he be voted a generous income in perpetuity. After Marlborough's victory at Blenheim, Anne dismissed his chief Tory critic, her uncle, the Earl of Rochester. Another Tory leader, Daniel Finch, 2nd Earl of Nottingham, resigned from his post of Secretary of State and was replaced by Robert Harley, who was also Speaker of

Battle of Blenheim by Romeyne de Hooghe, 1704. (Courtesy of Rijksmuseum, Amsterdam)

the Commons. Godolphin, Marlborough and Harley now became known as 'the Triumvirate'. After the general election of 1705, Anne dismissed more leading Tories and, under pressure from Sarah Churchill, appointed Sarah's son-in-law, the 3rd Earl of Sunderland, as ambassador in Vienna.

Anne was strongly influenced by personal likes and dislikes; she favoured Harley, a moderate Tory, but detested Sunderland, who was an extreme Whig, and she resented being forced by the Whigs to accept Sunderland as one of her Secretaries of State. Marlborough and Godolphin believed that the war against France could only be won if the support given to it by the Whigs in Parliament were reinforced by the presence of all the leading Whigs in the government. However, Harley preferred a central coalition government. Gradually, partly through the influence of Abigail Masham, one of Anne's favourite ladies-in-waiting, Harley came to exert so much influence over the queen that a rivalry developed between him and Godolphin. Anne was still dependent on Marlborough to win the war and so she was forced to dismiss Harley.

At the general election of May 1708, the Whigs won a majority in the Commons and Anne was compelled to admit members of what was known as the 'Whig Junto' into her Cabinet.

THE ACT OF UNION 1707

The 1701 Act of Settlement, which named the Protestant Hanoverian royal family as Anne's successors, had provoked anger in Scotland. The Act of Security of the kingdom, which the Scottish Parliament had passed in August 1703, demonstrated the Scots' willingness to bar the Hanoverian accession and raised the possibility that a Stuart king, most likely the Pretender, could be installed in Scotland and join forces with France against England. To prevent this, negotiations for the legal

ALL BEPATCHED

The Frenchman Monsieur Misson expressed his surprise that, unlike in his own country, English women wore patches until old age, commenting rather ungallantly that 'in England the young, handsome, ugly, all are bepatched till they are bed-rid. I have often counted fifteen patches, or more, upon the swarthy, wrinkled phiz of an old hag three score and ten upwards'.

Patches were made from silk, velvet and even paper and applied with mastic. Sometimes they were cut in the shape of silhouettes of family or friends and a prominent marquise was reported to have appeared at a party wearing sixteen patches, one in the shape of a tree on which were perched two birds. Patches were kept in boxes, usually rectangular, which were hinged and contained a small mirror inside the cover.

Patches took on a further significance as an indication of which political party a woman favoured. Somewhat surprisingly, Tory supporters patched on the left and Whigs on the right, while those who were uncertain patched on both sides. At an opera in 1711, a correspondent observed two parties of well-dressed women, seated on opposite side-boxes and commented, 'I perceived that they cast hostile glances upon each other and that their patches were placed in those different situations as party-signals to distinguish friends from foes.'

Patches were also useful for disguising blemishes, although those who were still concerned about the state of their skin could always resort to a preparation published in 1714, which claimed that it was 'A Certain Cure for Scabs, Pimples and the Old Inveterate Itch'. As this contained flowers of brimstone, butter and red precipate, fashionable ladies might have preferred to use the following, which was advertised in *The London Post*.

The Venetian Wash, being a Most Excellent Water, to beautify and add loveliness to the face, by taking out all freckles, sun-brown and yellowness. 1 shilling a bottle.

Opposite: The magnificent Blenheim Palace at Woodstock, Oxfordshire, was the home of John Churchill, 1st Duke of Marlborough and his wife Sarah. Given as a gift by Queen Anne after Marlborough's victory at Blenheim in 1704, the building of the house involved many of the finest architects of the day, including Sir John Vanbrugh, and took many years to complete. (Copyright David P. Howard. Courtesy of Blenheim Palace)

*John Churchill, Duke of
Marlborough*, attributed
to Johann Friedrich Ardin.
(Courtesy of Rijksmuseum,
Amsterdam)

union of England and Scotland began formally in 1706 and on 22 July of that year,
a draft treaty was agreed by the sixty-two appointed commissioners. The treaty
provided for a united kingdom with a single Parliament in Westminster, a single
currency, a common union flag and a guaranteed Protestant succession to the
Hanoverian royal line. In addition, it provided for the Scottish Church, education
and legal systems to be independent of those in England. Despite riots in Glasgow,
the Act of Union was passed by the Scottish Parliament on 16 January 1707; its
passage was smoothed by a payment of £400,000 and innumerable bribes.

The Act received royal assent in Westminster on 6 March 1707, and at a
thanksgiving service on 1 May at the recently completed St Paul's Cathedral, Anne
wore the insignia of the combined Order of the Garter and Order of the Thistle.

THE END OF A FRIENDSHIP

Within a few years of becoming queen, Anne's relationship with Sarah Churchill,
Duchess of Marlborough, began to sour. Sarah became more critical and assertive,

and when she realised that she was being supplanted by Abigail Masham, a lady of the bedchamber, her rages became worse. The differences were not only personal but political; Anne was a committed Anglican and was inclined to Toryism, although she disliked party politics and was keen to promote national unity. Sarah, however, was a fierce Whig, asserting that all Tories were Jacobites.

Sarah's anger against the Tories was increased by their growing disenchantment with the war, which soon hardened into opposition. This was partly because the land tax raised to pay for the war bore heavily on Tory squires and only the City of London and the great Whig families connected with the money power derived any benefit from continued hostilities. Moreover, the Tories believed that the war was being fought in the interests of the Dutch and the Habsburg emperor and not of England. As the Tories turned against the war and therefore against Marlborough himself, Sarah's attachment to the Whigs increased, as did her rages with the queen.

Invasion Fears

1708 proved to be a difficult and painful year for Anne. Early in the year, Louis XIV provided a French invasion fleet for Anne's half-brother, the twenty-year-old James Francis Edward Stuart. While Anne, immobile again with gout, waited anxiously at Kensington, measures were put into place to meet the threatened invasion, including a proclamation declaring the Pretender and all his supporters to be rebels. Catholics were under suspicion and the Abjuration oath was re-administered. However, the invasion was delayed when the prince became ill with measles and he was intercepted by the fleet of Admiral Sir George Byng when he attempted to land at the Firth of Forth on 23 March 1708. The French Admiral, Claude Fourbin, refused to land the Pretender, choosing to retreat rather than risk a naval battle. A plan to sail north to Inverness was frustrated by storms, and the expedition returned to Dunkirk.

Prince George became seriously ill, and Anne spent many nights holding him up in her arms to help him breathe. Anne was cheered by news of Marlborough's victory at Oudenarde in August, but her husband's health continued to deteriorate and he died on 28 October, to Anne's overwhelming sorrow.

Although the prince had been a figure of fun to many, he had been Anne's faithful supporter and companion for twenty-five years, being content to remain in the background and loving 'his news, his bottle and the Queen'.

Feeling that she could no longer trust any members of her government, Anne's sense of isolation and loneliness was compounded by her increasing alienation from Sarah Churchill, who absented herself for long periods from her duties at court and devoted herself to pro-Whig propaganda.

'I AM STILL FOR MODERATION AND WILL GOVERN BY IT'

By 1709, the kingdom was weary of the long and costly war and although Marlborough achieved another victory at Malplaquet, the losses of the Allies were heavier than those of the French.

Anne was concerned that the Church was in danger, particularly as she was not allowed to appoint the bishops of her choice, who were usually High Churchmen. In February 1710 a clergyman named Henry Sacheverell was impeached in Westminster Hall after delivering an outspoken attack on Dissenters, toleration and the Whig settlement after the Revolution of 1688. Although found guilty, Sacheverell's punishment was extremely light, provoking a political reaction. Determined to stir up fears that religious toleration threatened the Church of England, he began a campaign which was supported by clergy throughout the country.

Secretly in touch with Harley, Anne dismissed Godolphin, an action she was later to regret. The pro-Anglican and anti-war sentiments were expressed in the general election of 1710, which resulted in an overwhelming Tory victory under the leadership of Robert Harley.

At the beginning of the following year, amid painful scenes, Anne finally dismissed Sarah from all her offices and dismissed Marlborough by the end of the year. Harley took office and another Tory, the able and ambitious Henry, St John Viscount Bolingbroke, secured a peace with France. To ensure that both Houses of Parliament approved the peace, Anne agreed to create twelve additional Tory peers.

When she opened Parliament in 1713, the queen was able to inform the members of the Treaty of Utrecht. In the general election that followed, the Tories were again victorious. However, Harley's powers were failing and Anne dismissed him from office in July 1713. Distrusting Bolingbroke, the queen appointed her old friend, the Whiggish Earl of Shrewsbury, as Lord Treasurer.

THE END OF AN ERA

By 1713, Anne's health, never good, began to deteriorate. Rumours about the queen's attitude to the succession began to circulate, for although Anne had publicly acknowledged the Hanoverian succession, her dislike of them was no secret. Stories were spread that the queen had left a will contravening the Act and that she intended to invite King James II's son, the Pretender, to share her throne. It is possible that Anne experienced some feelings of guilt over her desertion of her father, the king, and her part in promoting the rumours that her half-brother James was illegitimate. However, she had refused to reply to a long letter from James in which he attempted to resolve their differences.

For the first seven months of 1713 Anne was unable to walk, and she was too ill to attend the celebrations for the signing of the Treaty of Utrecht. In December, she caught a severe chill, lying unconscious for several hours, while rumours of her death and an imminent invasion of the Pretender provoked panic. Anne survived, but her health and spirits remained poor. On 8 June 1714, the Electress Sophia, the heir to throne, collapsed and died.

Queen Anne died on 1 August 1714. She had been ill for several days and patiently endured the painful treatments of her physicians and the bickering of her ministers who crowded around her bed. The queen's doctor, John Arbuthnot, commented that 'I believe sleep was never more welcome to a weary traveller than death was to her'.

With Anne's death, the House of Stuart came to an end, and Prince George of Hanover ascended the throne as George I.

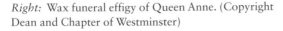

Above: Original silver mounted lodestone reputed to have been used by Queen Anne during healing ceremonies at the Banqueting House, as the queen disliked touching her subjects directly. It was believed that a monarch's power could heal the 'king's evil', scrofula. (Courtesy of Wellcome Library, London)

Right: Wax funeral effigy of Queen Anne. (Copyright Dean and Chapter of Westminster)

WHAT NEXT?

FICTION

Davis, Lindsey, *Rebels and Traitors*
Gregory, Philippa, *Earthly Joys*
Gregory, Philippa, *Virgin Earth*
McCann, Maria, *As Meat Loves Salt*
Womack, P. J., *Darling of Kings*
Zuvich, Andrea, *His Last Mistress: The Duke of Monmouth and Lady Henrietta Wentworth*

NON-FICTION

Adamson, Jon, *The Noble Revolt; The overthrow of Charles I* (Wiedenfeld & Nicolson, 2007)
Brears, Peter C.D., *Stuart Cookery: Recipes and History* (Cooking Through the Ages) (English Heritage: Revised edition, 2004)
Brandon, David, *Life in a Seventeenth-Century Coffee Shop* (The Sutton Life Series) (The History Press, 2007)
Froome, Joyce, *A History of the Pendle Witches and Their Magic: Wicked Enchantments* (Palatine Books, 2010)
Harris, Tim, *Rebellion: Britain's First Stuart Kings, 1567–1642* (Oxford University Press, 2014)
Latham Pepys, Robert, *The Illustrated Pepys: Extracts from the Diary of Samuel Pepys* (Book Club Associates: Guild Publishing, 1979)
Valance, Edward, *The Glorious Revolution: 1688 – Britain's Fight for Liberty* (Little, Brown & Company, 2006)

TV

Charles II: The Power & the Passion (2003)
Gunpowder Treason and Plot (2004)
New Worlds (2014)
The Devil's Whore (2008)
The Musketeers (2014)

FILMS

Cromwell (1970)
Stage Beauty (2004)
The Draughtsman's Contract (1982)
To Kill a King (2003)
The Libertine (2004)
The Serpent's Kiss (1997)

INDEX

Also in the Illustrated Introductions series

Fascinated by history? Wish you knew more?
The Illustrated Introductions are here to help.

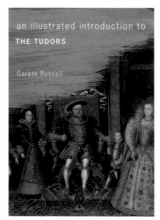

An Illustrated Introduction to the
Tudors
978-1-4456-4121-8
£9.99
Available from October 2014

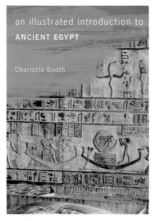

An Illustrated Introduction to
Ancient Egypt
978-1-4456-3365-7
£9.99

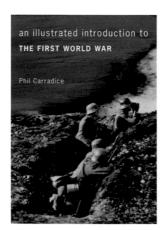

An Illustrated Introduction to the
First World War
978-1-4456-3296-4
£9.99

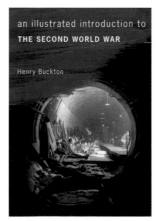

An Illustrated Introduction to the
Second World War
978-1-4456-3848-5
£9.99

Available from all good bookshops or to order direct
Please call **01453-847-800**
www.amberleybooks.com